普通高等教育"十二五"规划教材

全国高职高专规划教材·会展策划与管理系列

实用会展英语(第二版)

Practical English for Conference & Exhibition (Second Edition)

主　编　邱玉华

参　编　梁　爽　张　莲

图书在版编目(CIP)数据

实用会展英语/邱玉华主编. —2 版. —北京：北京大学出版社，2014.4
(全国高职高专规划教材·会展策划与管理系列)
ISBN 978-7-301-23999-5

Ⅰ. ①实⋯　Ⅱ. ①邱⋯　Ⅲ. ①展览会－英语－高等学校－教材　Ⅳ. ①H31

中国版本图书馆 CIP 数据核字(2014)第 041715 号

书　　名：	实用会展英语(第二版)
著作责任者：	邱玉华　主　编
责 任 编 辑：	胡伟晔
标 准 书 号：	ISBN 978-7-301-23999-5/H·3488
出 版 发 行：	北京大学出版社
地　　　址：	北京市海淀区成府路 205 号　100871
网　　　址：	http://www.pup.cn　新浪官方微博：@北京大学出版社
电 子 信 箱：	zyjy@pup.cn
电　　　话：	邮购部 62752015　发行部 62750672　编辑部 62765126　出版部 62754962
印　刷　者：	北京圣夫亚美印刷有限公司
经　销　者：	新华书店
	787 毫米×1092 毫米　16 开本　9.75 印张　234 千字
	2009 年 7 月第 1 版
	2014 年 4 月第 2 版　2022 年 7 月第 5 次印刷　总第 7 次印刷
定　　　价：	25.00 元

未经许可，不得以任何方式复制或抄袭本书之部分或全部内容。

版权所有，侵权必究

举报电话：010-62752024　电子信箱：fd@pup.pku.edu.cn

前　言

本书在2009年出版的《实用会展英语》的基础上进行改编和增补，把第1单元中国的会展介绍扩展到了对世界会展及中国会展的介绍，并增加了第8单元会展行业入职准备，详细介绍了目前中国提供的几种权威的会展资格考试和会展行业从业资质，这是目前市面上的英语教材很少涉及的内容。

本书侧重培养学生用英语进行会展服务与接待的交际能力，以及会展整个流程中的策划、管理、营销、物流、谈判、设计及其他工作中的沟通能力，特别是口头表达能力。例如，书中交际活动不仅给出了情境，还提供了"Sample dialogue"，甚至列出学生在具体的每个情境里需要的词汇和表达方式，帮助学生适应全球化发展趋势和提高与国外参展商打交道的能力。

考虑到与学生相关的就业前景，本书编者一直坚持从会展业中的两大主要参与者——组展商和参展商的立场来编写。例如，第3单元"会展筹备"就分为第1节"组展方的准备工作"（如策划主题、提供的服务、会议安排）和第2节"参展方的准备工作"（如电话咨询、报名、预订展位和酒店房间）；第4单元"参展"包括第1节"布展：展台搭建和接待"，第2节"展品推介、会展服务及组团参展"，以及第3节"会展期间突发情况"。这些章节涉及的内容从一次展会的开始筹备到最后总结阶段，对于一名会展从业人员来说，这些内容都是在日常的工作中所涉及的，能够切实为学生将来的就业提供帮助。

本书材料的选取既有知识性，又有很强的现代感和国际性，有助于拓宽学生视野。本书增加了会展背景知识的内容，以国内会展为主导，辅之以相应的国外内容。因为会展英语不仅是语言能力的培养，也是文化意识的培养。只有了解这些文化背景知识，才能更好地应对工作中出现的种种情况。

本书由重庆第二师范学院邱玉华副教授任主编，负责整体策划，制定单元框架和编写体例，构思各单元内容并审定全稿。其中，邱玉华负责第1、第2和第7单元的编写；张莲负责第3和第5单元的编写；梁爽负责第4、第6和第8单元的编写。校稿人为加拿大外籍教师Fraser Fell（弗雷泽·费尔）和英国朋友Nick Weller（尼克·韦勒），在此对他们表示衷心的感谢。

纵有良好愿望和百般努力，疏漏和不妥之处亦在所难免，恳请广大读者指正赐教，以待修订补足。

本教材配有教学课件，如有老师需要，请发电子邮件至zyjy@pup.cn或加QQ群（279806670）索取，也可致电北京大学出版社：010-62765126。

编　者
2013年10月

Contents
目　　录

Unit 1　Introduction of MICE Industry at Home and Abroad 国内外会展业概况 ······················1
　Lesson 1　Introduction of the World MICE Industry 世界会展业概况·····························2
　Lesson 2　Yesterday and Today of China's MICE Industry 中国会展业的历史和现状···········10

Unit 2　Exhibition and Conference Centers in China 中国的会展中心 ·······························18
　Lesson 1　Size and Location of Exhibition Centers 会展中心的面积与位置······················19
　Lesson 2　Space Size and Location 展台面积与位置···26

Unit 3　Preparations for the Exhibition 会展筹备 ···36
　Lesson 1　Preparations by the Host 组展方的准备工作··37
　Lesson 2　Preparations by the Exhibitors 参展方的准备工作·······································45

Unit 4　Participation in an Exhibition 参展 ···54
　Lesson 1　Decorating: Stand Construction and Reception 布展：展台搭建和接待·············55
　Lesson 2　Promotion of Exhibits, Services Provided and Delegations 展品推介、会展服务及组团参展······61
　Lesson 3　Emergencies during the Exhibition 会展期间突发情况···································68

Unit 5　Cancellation and Move-out 退展和撤展 ··77
　Lesson 1　Cancellation of Exhibit Registration 取消预订展位·······································78
　Lesson 2　Move-out 撤展···85

Unit 6　Post-Conference Tour 会后游···94

Unit 7　Exhibition and Conference Strategies 会展策略 ··104
　Lesson 1　Organizers' Strategies 组展方的策略···105
　Lesson 2　Exhibitors' Strategies 参展商的策略···111

Unit 8　Preparations for the MICE Profession 会展行业入职准备 ····································119
　Lesson 1　Career Prospect of MICE 会展行业职业前景···120
　Lesson 2　Qualifications for the MICE Profession 会展行业职业资格····························126

参考答案···136
参考文献···150

Unit 1

Introduction of MICE Industry at Home and Abroad

国内外会展业概况

单元目标

1. 了解 2012 年韩国举行的世博会。
2. 了解世界（欧美发达国家及亚洲发展中国家）会展业的发展及分布情况，以及最近几年的发展特征和趋势。
3. 了解中国会展业的发展和现状、特点、分类及发展趋势。
4. 关注所在城市的各种形式的会展，了解组展的原因和动力。
5. 了解世界会展业的产生背景和重要的主展国家。

Lesson 1

Introduction of the World MICE Industry
世界会展业概况

Section I A Sample Dialogue

[Scene] Peter and Wang are talking about the significance of World Expo and they feel amazed at its impact and development. They take delight in talking about the latest World Expo held in the coastal city of Yeosu in South Korea in 2012. The theme of the Expo is "Living Ocean and Coast", aiming to maintain and develop natural resources.

Peter 和 Wang 在谈论世博会的意义。他们对世博会的影响和发展感到惊讶,并且对2012年在韩国丽水举办的主题为"生机勃勃的海洋及海岸"、探讨资源多样性与可持续发展的世博会津津乐道。

Peter: Wang, do you know what the world's three greatest festivals are?

Wang: They are the Olympics, FIFA World Cup and …what is the third one?

Peter: It's the World Exposition or World Expo, also known as World's Fair. It is the third largest event in the world, in terms of economic and cultural impact. World Expo has a history longer than both the modern Olympic Games and the World Cup.

Wang: Indeed it is. Nowadays Expo is the word on everyone's lips. What is the World Expo, then?

Peter: Well, the World Expo is a global, non-commercial exposition held in different countries in the world. It aims at promoting the exchange of ideas, development of production over the world, and also improving the international relations.

Wang: When and where was it started?

Peter: So far as I know, the first World Expo was held in London on May 1, 1851. It lasted for 160 days. By the way, do you know anything about the latest World Expo?

Unit 1 Introduction of MICE Industry at Home and Abroad 国内外会展业概况

Wang: I saw on TV that it was held in South Korea.

Peter: Yes, the latest was held in the coastal city of Yeosu in South Korea, from May 12 to August 12.

Wang: It lasted 3 months. Quite long, wasn't it? Why was it held? I mean, what was the purpose of holding it?

Peter: It aimed at shining a spotlight on the global benefits of maintaining our oceans, to find solutions to climate change, to stop depletion of natural resources and the destruction of the ecosystem.

Wang: I heard that its theme was related to ocean.

Peter: "Living Ocean and Coast" was its theme. Over 100 nations including China, Egypt, the UAE, Russia, Germany and the US, as well as 10 international organizations such as the UNESCO Intergovernmental Oceanographic Commission took part in it.

Wang: Wow, it was really eye-catching. Tell me something interesting about it, please.

Peter: The center piece of the 2012 site was the 40-metre high "Big-O" structure. It comprised the world's largest over-the-sea fountain, and the Aquarium is the largest in South Korea with 34,000 marine species in the 6.03-tonne tank.

Wang: What happened to the exhibition structures after the expo?

Peter: The exhibition structures were all temporary structures. Most of the buildings were already sold to national and international organizations. Some remain standing there for tourism. For example, the "Big-O" structure, along with the Theme Pavilion and Aquarium, remain after the expo closed in August.

Wang: What benefits did the host country get from holding the expo?

Peter: A lot. To name a few, first, it has driven the development of South Korea's south coast and helped to accelerate the nation's marine industry and technology. Second, it has delivered an economic impact of $5.3bn and generated 80,000 new jobs.

Wang: No doubt, the World Expo is a big global festival.

Peter: Absolutely. The next one will be held in 2015 in Milan. Let's wait and see what it will be like.

1. Read the conversation again and decide whether the following statements are true (T) or false (F).

(1) Generally speaking, the world's greatest festivals are those events that catch the world's attention. ( )

(2) The purpose of World Expo is not to make money, but to exchange human ideas and inspirations about science, economy, culture and so on. ( )

(3) Both the first World Expo held in 1851 and the latest expo in 2012 were long-term expositions, because they lasted over one week. ( )

(4) The theme of the Yeosu World Expo was "Living Ocean and Coast", which aimed at drawing the world's attention to ocean protection and global climate change. ( )

(5) The 40-metre high "Big-O" structure, the center piece of the 2012 site, formed the world's largest fountain over the sea. （　）

(6) All exhibition structures are temporary for the show and they are torn down after the show. （　）

(7) Although World Expos don't aim at making money, the host countries usually can get a lot of benefits from holding the world expos, including monetary benefits. （　）

(8) Yeosu, where the 2012 World Expo was held, was the only city benefited from this World Expo in South Korea. （　）

2．In groups, discuss what is "会展".

For example, in a narrow sense, "会展" is understood as convention & exhibition industry. In a broad sense, it is understood as MICE industry. What is included in its narrow and broad sense respectively? Find out the related events from the given chart below.

Cultural Celebration (文化庆典)	festival(节日)
	carnivals(狂欢节)
	religious events(宗教事件)
	parades(大型展演)
	heritage commemorations(历史纪念活动)
Art/Entertainment (文艺/娱乐事件)	concerts(音乐会)
	other performances(其他表演)
	exhibits(文艺展览)
	award ceremonies(授奖仪式)
Business/Trade (商贸事件)	fairs,markets,sales(展览会、集市、展销会)
	consumer and trade shows(交易会)
	expositions(博览会)
	meetings and conventions(会议)
	publicity events(广告促销)
	fund-raiser events(募捐)
Sport Competitions (体育赛事)	professional(职业比赛)
	amateur(业余竞赛)
Educational and Science (教科事件)	seminars,workshops,clinics(研讨班、专题学术会议、学术讨论会)
	congresses(学术大会)
	interpretive events(教科阐释解释会)
Recreational (休闲事件)	games and sports for fun(游戏和趣味体育)
	amusement events(娱乐事件)
Political/State (政治/政府事件)	inaugurations(就职典礼)
	investitures(授职/授勋仪式)
	VIP visits(贵宾观礼)
	rallies(群众集会)

续表

Private Events (私人事件)	personal celebrations(个人庆典)
	anniversaries(周年纪念)
	family holidays(家庭聚会)
	rites de passage(宗教礼拜)
Social Events (社交事件)	parties,galas(舞会、节日)
	reunions de passage(同学/亲友联欢会)

3. Match the jargons on the left with the Chinese equivalents on the right.

(1) festival 　　　　　　　　　　　a. 主办国
(2) non-commercial exposition　　　　b. 会展业
(3) MICE industry　　　　　　　　　c. 节庆，节事活动
(4) host country　　　　　　　　　　d. 参加者
(5) convention/conference　　　　　　e. 国内/国外(会议/展览)场所
(6) attendee　　　　　　　　　　　　f. 会议
(7) exhibition structures　　　　　　　g. 参展建筑物
(8) destination　　　　　　　　　　　h. 奖励旅游
(9) domestic/overseas venue　　　　　i. 非商业性质的博览/非营利的博览
(10) incentive trip/tour　　　　　　　 j. 目的地

Section II Communication Activities

1. Pair Work

Take turns asking and answering the following questions with a partner.

(1) Why is the MICE industry an indispensable part of the business world?

Answer: Well, it will take a while to answer this. Let's just take conferences for an example. It is understood that businesses and associations simply cannot function in a fully effective way without face-to-face meetings. It is also understood that conferences and incentive travel are an indispensable means of communicating their business messages, increasing sales, and business development.

(2) Is the MICE industry developing all over the world?

Answer: Yes, it is developing globally. But the development pace is not the same. For example, Europe and the States have already had years of experience and achievement, while in many developing countries, such as China, this industry is still new. This means that there are plenty of opportunities for this industry to grow in these developing countries.

(3) Is the MICE industry influenced by the recent global economic slowdown?

Answer: Yes, it has been hard in recent years, but there are also many points for optimism. For example, in the year of 2012, the World Tourism Organization data shows that there are more people travelling than ever. Data also shows that there is continuing investment in the development and promotion of many of the MICE facilities and services.

(4) Among meetings, incentive travel, conventions and events, which has the biggest development potential, according to your knowledge?

Answer: Personally speaking, I think incentive trips are to grow fast. I believe the family market for business travel, events and incentives will continue to grow. Nowadays, executives who are working longer hours, are looking for ways to balance work and family. Plenty of data shows increasing numbers of conference delegates are bringing their children along when travelling.

2．Role Play

Student A: A spokesperson at an international conference is talking about the history and prospect of World Expos.

Student B, C, D…: Reporters from different countries.

[**Sample dialogue**]

A: Distinguished guests, ladies and gentlemen, reporters from the media, welcome to this conference on promoting World Expos to the world. It is truly a pleasure for me to speak at the 7th World Expo International Forum. The series of World Expo International Forums are important events to promote the ideal of the World Expo and expand its influence. Participants to this forum will have extensive and in-depth discussions. Before the discussion I'd like to offer you background information about the past, the present, and even the future of World Expos. Now, here comes your turn to ask some relevant questions.

B: Good morning, Mr. A. I'm…, the reporter from *China Daily*. I would like to get some information about…

C: Hello, I'm from the British Broadcasting Corporation. Just now you mentioned…in your speech, I would like to ask you to talk more about the details.

D: Thank you for giving me the opportunity to ask you a question. I'm…from the *Morning Post* in America. My question is...

Reporters	Spokesperson
When was the World Expo first started?	The first Expo was held in the Crystal Palace in London, in 1851 under the title "Great Exhibition of the Works of Industry of All Nations". It was the idea of Prince Albert, Queen Victoria's husband. The first Expo influenced the development of many aspects of society.
What are the developmental stages of World Expo?	The character of World Expo has evolved in three eras: the era of industrialization(1851～1938), the era of cultural exchange(1939～1987), and the era of nation branding(1988～present).
How many World Expos have been held by now?	So far, over 40 World Expositions have been held in the world.
What is the significance of competing for the chance to host World Expos?	A host country of World Expos can benefit a lot. Today's World Expositions include elements of all three eras. Host countries can present new inventions, show their products and skills, and promote the branding of the host city, region and nation.

Unit 1 Introduction of MICE Industry at Home and Abroad 国内外会展业概况

续表

Reporters	Spokesperson
What are the new development trends of World Expos?	The early World Expos used to worship economic progress, but in recent years, World Expos focus more on sustainable development and concepts alike. For example, the World Expo in 2000 in Hanover listed environmental protection in the topics for discussion. The theme of 2005 Aichi World Expo is "Nature's Wisdom". Five years later, 2010 Shanghai World Expo in China, with the theme "Better City, Better Life", explored harmonious city life.

Section Ⅲ Expansion Reading

[导读]

会展业越来越成熟、越来越专业。科技进步影响了这个行业，不管是展览还是会议，甚至是奖励旅游都出现了新的发展趋势。2008 年开始并持续至今的世界经济的不景气给会展业提出一个需要思考的问题：展销会该在国内开还是走出国门去开？不同的国家就这个问题给出了不同的答案。

New Development Trends in the Global MICE Industry

The MICE (standing for meetings, incentives, conventions and events / exhibitions respectively) industry has been a growing industry over the past few decades into a mature business sector, driven by growing professional world.

1. Advances in Technology and Their Impacts

Organizing a meeting or incentive trip involves moving around vast amounts of information. This is something that computers and the Internet can do very effectively. No one doubts that the use of technology by the MICE industry will continue to expand, transforming the way meeting and incentive travels are organized. The Internet is already a valuable source for promoting services and facilities on offer from venues, hotels, and destinations. Also online booking tools will continue to help planners and suppliers work more effectively, and events management software has evolved from merely providing information , about events to enabling full online management of a conference.

2. Principal Trends of Meetings and Incentive Travels

The new trend of meetings is that they are becoming shorter and smaller, with less delegates as companies have tough controls on their conference-related spending. The weak economy has led many companies to cut meeting budgets. With limited time and budgets, business delegates only want to attend those events which are really in need.

However, growing indications show that meetings are being held more frequently, because the rapid changes in business and society as a whole means that companies and corporations have to hold more meetings and events , so that their members or employees can keep up with the fast-moving changes in their field or profession.

Likewise, in the incentive travel sector, cost-cutting measures also have hit incentive budgets hard, and the constant threat of uncertainty has meant that incentive planners, more than ever, need to confirm that a destination is safe before they will even begin to consider it.

As a result, the design and nature of many incentive programs has changed. Many incentive programs have been held in destinations nearer to the participants' homes. The average number of participants per incentive group is shrinking, and incentive trip organizers have to include more flexibility and "free time arrangement" to save expense.

3. The Option of Domestic Venue or Overseas Venue

During the tough economic environment beginning in 2008, the MICE sector has faced the difficult choice of whether to hold corporate events in the domestic market, or to spend big money overseas to attract attendees.

For example, figures from a survey of corporations in the UK throughout 2009 showed that 47% of businesses imposed restrictions on overseas travel, with 83% admitting to holding their events in the UK. London was by far the biggest winner from this, with 60% of organizations saying that the city was the most used in 2009.

In the US, it is different and the international expansion is still seen as the best route to business success. The annual amount spent on marketing to overseas attendees has seen the greatest rise for 2012. Almost a quarter (23%) of survey respondents say they spent 10% more than last year on attracting overseas attendees. 39% of organizers are currently holding events outside the US, with 46% in the process of taking their events out of the country. The majority of these events are currently taking place in China (23%), South America (14%) and the UK (10%). India, Singapore and Dubai are three other countries favoured by 18%, 12% and 9% of US organizers respectively.

1. Make the best choice according to the passage.

(1) What are the contributing factors to the growth of MICE industry?
A. Computers.　　B. Internet.　　C. Cell phones.　　D. All of the above.

(2) The new trend of meetings is for meeting to be _____.
A. shorter　　B. smaller　　C. more frequent　　D. All of the above.

(3) The chief reason for the new trend of meetings is _____.
A. saving time　　B. tight budgets　　C. no demand　　D. All of the above.

(4) The new trend of incentive travel includes _____.
A. shrinking　　B. tight budgets　　C. security　　D. All of the above.

(5) What is the main reason for the new trend of incentive tour?
A. Uncertainty.　　　　　　　　B. Rapid changes in business.
C. Tight budgets.　　　　　　　D. Safety.

(6) The chief cause of the new trends of the world MICE industry is _____.
A. rapid changes　　　　　　　B. scientific advances
C. tough economic situation　　D. globalization

(7) British MICE organizers tend to prefer _____ as venues to hold exhibitions and conferences.

A. overseas　　　　　　　　B. Europe

C. the domestic market　　　D. developing countries

(8) _____ of US organizers are now holding events in other countries.

A. 39%　　　B. 10%　　　C. 23%　　　D. 46%

2. Translate the following sentences using as many language skills learned in this lesson as possible.

(1) 组织会议或奖励旅游涉及运作大量的信息。

(2) 会议的发展趋势：变短变小，但是更频繁。

(3) 奖励旅游的趋势：团队规模缩小，就近旅游，并且多安排自由活动。

(4) 经济萧条使会展业面临着是组织国内展还是走出国门去吸引参展商的艰难选择。

(5) 虽然英国人更趋向于国内组展，但是美国人仍在国外花大笔钱，把国际扩展策略当作会展业发展之道。

Section Ⅳ　The Internet Research

1. What is the historical background of world exhibitions? What are the goals of exhibitions?

2. Which parties (sides) are involved in an exhibition? What are their relationships like?

3. What happens to the architectures especially built for an exhibition after the event? Do they become permanent structures?

Section Ⅴ　New Words You've Met in This Lesson

spotlight	n.	公众注意或突出显著
ecosystem	n.	生态系统
theme	n.	主题；主旋律
comprise	vt.	包含，包括；由……组成
temporary	adj	临时的，暂时的；短暂的
incentive	adj./n.	刺激性的；鼓励性质的；激励某人做某事的事物；刺激；动机
transform	vt./vi.	改变；改观
venue	n.	会场，地点
principal	adj.	最重要的；主要的
delegate	n.	代表；代表团
corporation	n.	公司
destination	n.	目的地
option	n.	选择
impose…on	vt.	强加；征税
respondent	N	回答者
respectively	adv.	各自地，分别地

Lesson 2

Yesterday and Today of China's MICE Industry
中国会展业的历史和现状

Section I A Sample Dialogue

[Scene] Despite worldwide interest, China is not an easy market for new foreign companies to penetrate the exhibition industry due to cultural differences in doing business (for example, government red tape and a reliance on personal relationships with authorities and associations).

尽管中国会展是一块很大的市场，但外国组展公司要渗入这个行业非常不易，因为中国有特殊的生意经，如政府禁区、各个主管部门间的利益关系等。

以下是从事会展业的中国人 Wang 和从事相关行业的西方人 Thomas 的交流内容。

Thomas: Shanghai New International Exhibition Center (SNIEC) is a fantastic example of cooperation between foreign companies and the Chinese government in the field of exhibition industry.

Wang: Yes, indeed. It's a joint venture of Messe Dusseldorf, Messe Hannover, Messe Munchen, and China's Shanghai Putong Land Development Corporation.

Thomas: The terms "exhibition", "trade fair", "fair", and "expo" used in China and Europe have little difference in meaning from the terms "trade show" and "show" used in the USA. But doing business in China is not easy for a foreign exhibition company due to our cultural differences.

Wang: Really? Can you give some examples?

Thomas: UFI (The Global Association of the Exhibition Industry) officially defines international exhibitions as those exhibitions with foreign exhibitors making up at least 10% of the total number of exhibitors, or with 5% relevant foreign visitors of the total number of visitors. However, in China many organizers use the word "international" in their exhibition advertisements, even openly in their banners without considering whether they can reach these standards.

Wang: Well, that's an eye-catching way to attract attention and attendance.

Thomas: In the western world, not every show is open to any visitor. An example of this would be a trade exhibition. A trade exhibition, or a trade show, means a consumer/public exhibition that is open to trade professionals and not to the public.

Unit 1　Introduction of MICE Industry at Home and Abroad 国内外会展业概况

**　　　　　　**Normally, a member of the public can pay a fee to enter a consumer exhibition, while a visitor to a trade exhibition must be invited or have trade professional identification, and pay a higher entrance fee than would be charged for a public exhibition. Many trade exhibitions do not allow public visitors, even if they are willing to pay, but it seems that in China anybody can visit any show if they are willing to pay the entrance fees. There is no limit to visitors.

Wang:　　Well, it's a pity. We do differ a lot in this respect.

Thomas: Due to an oversupply of exhibition centers, many less-used exhibition centers are offering big rental discounts to attract more exhibitions. Sometimes we find it's hard to believe how much the same center's rental cost differs within the same year, sometimes even in the same month. Such a move is not helpful in the long run.

Wang:　　Yes, this practice certainly causes ill competition. It's nice talking with you. I am now able to realize the differences in our practice.

1. Answer the following questions orally according to the dialogue.

(1) Why is China not an easy market in terms of the exhibition industry?

(2) Who are the cooperative parties of SNIEC?

(3) What does Thomas imply by "The terms 'exhibition', 'trade fair', 'fair', and 'expo' used in China and Europe have little difference in meaning from the terms 'trade show' and 'show' used in the USA?"

(4) What are the standards of an international event in the exhibition industry?

(5) When Chinese organizers use the world "international" in their ads, are they aware of the standards?

(6) Is it a common practice for Chinese organizers to permit entrance as long as entrance fees are paid? What is the case in western countries?

(7) Why do some centers offer big rental discounts?

(8) What is the consequence of dramatically changing rental prices too often?

2. Discuss in groups.

The main aim of an exhibition is to create business opportunities between the exhibitors and trade visitors (or trade buyers). To organize a conference or an exhibition is a huge project which involves a lot of work and a lot of people. In groups, brainstorm to sum up "who are the parties involved in the exhibition industry" and use a web diagram to describe how they are related(关系). Also answer the following questions.

(1) Who are the major parties of a convention/an exhibition event?

(2) What are the relationships among the parties that exist in an exhibition event?

3. Match the jargons on the left with the Chinese equivalents on the right.

(1) exhibition image   a. 合资企业
(2) professional conference organizer   b. 展览业
(3) exhibition industry   c. 会展形象
(4) joint venture   d. 参展商
(5) exhibitor   e. 面向公众开放的展览会/公共展
(6) consumer show/public show   f. 观众
(7) visitor   g. 入场券/入场费
(8) trade exhibition/fair   h. 租赁折扣/租用打折
(9) entrance fee   i. 专业会议组织者
(10) rental discounts   j. 贸易展

Section II Communication Activities

1. Pair Work

Please match the questions and answers. Take turns asking and answering the following questions with a partner.

Question List

( ) 1.	What do you think of China's exhibition industry?
( ) 2.	What important exhibitions held in China do you know?
( ) 3.	How does the Furniture China Show impress you?
( ) 4.	Do you have any suggestions on developing the exhibition industry in our country?
( ) 5.	Are you planning any events in China for next year?

Answer List

A. I know quite a few. The Furniture China Show in Shanghai is one example. The annual event has been held for 13 years and is now Asia's largest international furniture fair.

续表

B. The Chinese exhibition industry is prospering. The gap between Chinese and western exhibitors is also closing.

C. With the Chinese exhibition industry meeting international standards, it is probably the time for the government to let the industry prosper more on its own, without imposing too many regulations. This helps create real business value.

D. We are planning over 30 trade exhibitions on the mainland. Large, established events will grow steadily in important exhibition cities like Shanghai, Beijing and Guangzhou. And we will also launch new events with new themes in second-tier cities like Chengdu, Suzhou and Nanjing.

E. I did not expect it to be so international. I was very impressed to hear people speaking in English wherever I was at the event. China's exhibition industry is on a journey of long-term growth.

2. Role Play

A foreign reporter is interviewing a government official in charge of the MICE sector in Shenzhen.

[Sample dialogue]

Reporter: Mr. Wang, we know you have years of work experience in MICE. Would you mind answering some questions about the exhibition industry of your city?

Smith: My pleasure.

Reporter: My first question is…

Smith: …

Reporter: My second question is…

…

Reporter: Thank you for giving me the opportunity to ask you questions.

Reporter	Governmental official
the background of the MICE industry in Shenzhen	In the past, the city was not so open to the outside. Many people didn't even know what MICE was. Today, MICE is under great development.
the status quo (现状) of the MICE industry	It is booming/prospering/thriving at an amazing rate.
the prospect (前景) of the MICE industry	It is becoming the major contributor to the city's revenue; many companies are willing to attend them.
the potential (潜在空间) for development	It will strengthen purchasing power, population mobility, multicultural events, traffic flow, lower labour costs, etc.

Section Ⅲ　Expansion Reading

[导读]

中国会展业在最近十年得到了迅猛的发展。会展的本质是信息传播，它是联系参展商和观众的桥梁和纽带，已成为许多企业开展营销的重要方式。参展商、观众、组展方作为独立的利益个体，他们都要实现自己的利益。

The China National Convention Center

In today's fast-changing global market, the convention industry is a channel that provides business contacts and information at any time and any place. It is essential to industry traders and suppliers and it is proving important both as a bridge between science and culture, and as a window for promotion.

As a measure of the market economy, the exhibition industry has developed rapidly in the past 30 years since the reform and opening up in China. In 1992, there was one mega convention &exhibition center (over 50,000 square meters of indoor space) in China, totally 160,000 square meters. By 2003, there were 16 mega centers, totally 1,288,000 square meters, a growth of 705% in 11 years. The exhibition industry is a huge business. In 2005, the Chinese exhibition industry earned 12.75 billion ($1.6 billion) and achieved an annual growth rate of 18%. As a result of the recent convention and exhibition center building boom in China, many big Chinese cities are building huge new conference and exhibition centers. They have strong belief in the promise that the economic growth factor to the community is between 1∶10 to 1∶40 from direct exhibition income.

A typical example of the building boom is the 530,000-square-meter China National Convention Center close to Beijing's National Stadium and National Aquatics Center (known respectively as the "Bird's Nest" and the "Water Cube"). It is another recent addition to the capital's already impressive skyline. The center was the site of the Olympic main press center and international broadcasting center, and also the venue for the fencing and pistol shooting (part of the modern pentathlon) events. The complex includes a 6,400-square-meter conference hall, a 24,000-square-meter exhibition section, and a hotel of 443 guest rooms.

Conferences, along with seminars and discussions, also often involve banquets and accommodation. These functions increase a hotel's income, but also test the quality of its service management. Just one careless mistake within the complex arrangements necessary for such a function could ruin a hotel's reputation, sending it to the bottom of the competitive line. The managers of CNCC believe that attention to detail is what differentiates a good hotel from ordinary ones. As a result, the staff are asked to give 100% attention to every aspect of service to convention clients. For example, lights should be precisely angled so as to avoid casting a shadow on the speaker's face. Utmost flexibility from the hotel's existing facilities, conditions, and services are made use of in order to meet the specific needs of different conventions to be held at the hotel, such as political, commercial and academic conventions.

Contracts for international events in 2009 that the China National Convention Center has already secured include the 9th International Symposium on Salt, the World Heart Disease Convention, and the First World Mind Sports Games. It welcomes a busy year.

1. Read the passage again and decide whether the following statements are true (T) or false (F).

(1) The exhibition industry is a channel that provides business contacts and information to traders and suppliers. ( )

(2) The exhibition industry developed rapidly in the last 30 years as a measure of the Chinese planned economy. ( )

(3) In 1992, there was only one convention and exhibition center bigger than 30 000 square meters in Beijing. ( )

(4) By 2003, the total exhibition space in China had grown by more than 7 times. ( )

(5) The exhibition industry has brought large profits for the local economy; therefore, a lot of exhibition centers have been built in a lot of cities. ( )

(6) China National Convention Center lies close to the "Bird's Nest" and was made the place for the fencing and pistol shooting in the 2008 Beijing Olympic Games. ( )

(7) The managers urged staff members to give great attention to the details of service, thus the center distinguishes itself from other ordinary hotels. ( )

(8) The Center is awaiting a busy 2009 because a series of international events will be held there. ( )

2. Translate the following sentences using as many language skills learned in this lesson as possible.

(1) 会展业涉及较多的群体，主要有组展商、参展商、服务商、观众、赞助商等。

(2) 会展有不同的分类，如按照展会性质分可分为专业展、展销会和综合展。

(3) 会展按照展会间隔时间可以分为定期展和不定期展。

(4) 会展按参展商或观众的来源不同可分为国际展、国家展、地区展。

(5) 会展是为商品供应商、销售商等群体提供面对面的接触和商品信息的一个渠道。

Section Ⅳ　The Internet Research

(1) What are the major types of exhibition according to the properties of exhibits?

(2) How do you distinguish between domestic expos and international expos?

Section V New Words You've Met in This Lesson

penetrate	vt.	渗透
banner	n.	横幅
professional	n./adj.	专业人士；专业的；专业性的
prosper	vi.	繁荣，发展
second-tier city	n.	二线城市
multicultural	adj.	多种文化的，反映多种文化的
channel	n.	渠道，途径
mega	adj./n.	宏大的；精彩的；百万，巨大
launch	vt.	发起，开始从事
essential	adj.	必不可少的，绝对必要的
total	vt.	共计，总计
boom	n.	激增，繁荣，迅速发展
stadium	n.	体育馆，运动场
banquet	n.	宴会
accommodation	n.	食宿
reputation	n.	名气，名声，名誉
differentiate	vt.	区分，区别，辨别
angle	vt.	使……形成角度

Section VI Writing Related to EC Industry

Write a summary of the growth of China's exhibition and convention industry with at least 100 words. The following factors should be included: birth, present growth (ranking in the world in last two years), classification, trend, growth in major cities.

Section VII Review of This Unit

1. Jargons in This Unit

World Exposition/ Expo	世界博览会
theme pavilion	主题馆
MICE facilities	会展设施
meeting/conference budgets	会议预算
overseas travel	海外旅游
commercial exhibition	商业展

Unit 1 Introduction of MICE Industry at Home and Abroad 国内外会展业概况

续表

exhibition organizer	组展商
exhibition and conference (EC) industry	会议展览业
exhibition space	展场
exhibitors & visitors	参展商&观众
mega center	大型展览中心
conference, seminar, discussion, symposium	会议，专题研讨会，讨论会，研讨会
MICE industry	会展业
attendance	展览会人数(包括参展商和参观商等各种类型的人)
consumer show/public show	面向公众开放的展览会/公共展
contractor	服务供应商
rental discounts	租赁折扣/租用打折
commodity exhibition	商品交易展览
on-line application	网上报名

2. Sentence Patterns/Practical Dialogues

(1) …is the first/second/third largest event in the world, in terms of economic and cultural impact.

(2) It aims at promoting…, and also developing…

(3) Do you know anything about the latest…?

(4) The show covers…square meters accommodating …people.

(5) What happened to …?

(6) What are the new development trends of …?

(7) We do differ a lot in…

Unit 2

Exhibition and Conference Centers in China

中国的会展中心

单元目标

1. 了解中国会展业的迅猛发展势头：大中城市会展中心的修建、会展面积的扩大，以及明确细化的修建目的。
2. 了解国内的一些重要会展场所及其相关情况。
3. 认识会展中心除了面积和地理位置不同外，还有不同的展览领域/展览对象、不同的会展形象。
4. 学会阐释不同大小和位置的展台有不同的人流量，因而有不同的价位。
5. 学会用英文填写展位申请表，并能计算其收费，找到最佳的展位和价位。

Unit 2 Exhibition and Conference Centers in China 中国的会展中心

Lesson *1*

Size and Location of Exhibition Centers
会展中心的面积与位置

Section I A Sample Dialogue

[Scene] In class, a teacher is talking with the students about exhibition centers in their city Chongqing. The students have paid little attention to these venues and are made aware of the closeness of exhibition industry to their life.

课堂上，师生在谈论重庆当地的会展设施。学生们还没意识到自己周围有那么多会展设施，老师的提醒让他们对会展离自己的生活那么近有了更深的认识。

Teacher: Dear class, do you know how many exhibition and convention centers there are in our city?

Class: *(surprised)* Isn't there only one exhibition center in Chongqing?

Teacher: Which one?

Class: The Chongqing International Conference and Exhibition Center located on the south side of Changjiang River. In the same district as our college.

Teacher: You're partly correct. Let's review the definition of "exhibition and conference" together to have a better understanding of exhibition centers.

Student A: In a narrow sense, exhibition industry only refers to exhibitions and conferences.

Student B: At the very beginning of this course, the book tells us that in a broad sense, exhibition industry includes MICE. M stands for meeting, I stands for incentive tour, C stands for conference, and E stands for exhibition, exposition and event.

Teacher: Marvelous! "Event" entails a lot, such as cultural events, festivals, parades, recreational events, political events. Even if we are talking about exhibition industry in the narrow sense, we have more than 4 exhibition centers in this city, not to mention MICE in the broad sense.

(The class murmur.)

Teacher: Who lives in Shi Qiaopu?

Student C: I do.

Teacher: Inside the state-level high-tech development zone, very close to the starting point of Chongqing-Chengdu Expressway, there is a place that often holds nation-wide meetings, as well as international conferences. Have you heard of that place?

Student C: Yes, thanks for reminding me. I now recall that place is called Chongqing Exhibition Center. Since its completion in 1998, it has successfully held more than 200 exhibitions and conferences. For instance, the National High-tech Achievement Expo, and the International Three Gorges Travel Festival. It has two stadiums, one is round, and the other is square, covering 24,000 square meters in space. It can provide 1,250 standard indoor booths and other exhibition facilities, such as multi-function hall, cafes, VIP lounges, underground garages and outdoor space. My mother goes there to shop occasionally if there is a consumption goods exhibition.

Student A: I live in Yuzhong District, the very center of Chongqing city. In our district there are two famous conference venues. One is called Chongqing Yingguan International Conference and Exhibition Center, and the other is called Chongqing International Scientific Conference Center.

Student D: In Yubei District where I am from, there is a Chongqing Scientific Conference Center at No. 2, Xinji Road. When we pass by, we often see banners and signs of different meetings and conferences.

Teacher: You're right. All together there are over 6 professional exhibition and conference centers in our city at the present time. They specialize in different types and fields of exhibitions and conferences. For example, the one in Yang Jiaping is famous for holding exhibitions in the field of heavy industry products. That is to say, every exhibition center enjoys a different exhibition image, for they serve different exhibition purposes.

(The class smile and nod.)

Chongqing Exhibition Center at the High-tech Development Zone

1. Read the conversation again and decide whether the following statements are true (T) or false (F).

(1) Not everyone is clearly aware of the exhibition venues in the place where he/she lives.   ( )

(2) The exhibition and conference industry is far from our daily life. ( )

(3) In a narrow sense, exhibition industry only includes business and trade fairs, exhibitions and expositions. ( )

(4) The centers located in the same city enjoy similar exhibition images. ( )

(5) Exhibiting companies can choose any center as they like to host an event. ( )

(6) The teacher's re-explanation of the definition of MICE has made the students conscious of the venues in the city. ( )

(7) The center in Shi Qiaopu is very close to the start point of the Chongqing-Chengdu Expressway and thus has access to convenient and speedy transportation. ( )

(8) In order to display heavy industry products, such as bulldozers (推土机), steamer rollers (压路机) and trucks, exhibiting companies must find a center with outdoor space. ( )

2. Discuss in groups.

Sum up the reasons why exhibition centers are needed and how many professional centers there are in your city. Describe their respective exhibition images. For example, whether they are famous for heavy industry products/auto products/IT products exhibitions, whether they are well-known for its traffic convenience/spacious halls/first-class service, or well-known for holding conferences not products display, etc..

3. Match the jargons on the left with the Chinese equivalents on the right.

(1) booth area   a. 会议/展览中心
(2) booth personnel   b. 展台工作人员
(3) convention/exhibition center c. 摊位面积
(4) demonstrators   d. 展位上雇用的演示和讲解员
(5) exhibition facilities/venues e. 室外展场/展地
(6) location   f. 展览设施/场地
(7) incentive tour/festival g. 国家级会议/全国会议
(8) exposition   h. 地理位置
(9) nation-wide meeting   i. 博览会
(10) outdoor space   j. 奖励旅游/节庆活动

Section Ⅱ Communication Activities

1. Pair Work

Look at the chart and take turns asking and answering questions with a partner.

[Sample dialogue]

A: How big is the … International Conference and Exhibition Center?

B: It covers an area of around 64,000 square meters.

实用会展英语(第二版)

Name	Size	Location	Facilities
Chongqing International Conference and Exhibition Center	It consists of indoor and outdoor exhibition spaces, covering a total area of about 64,000 square meters.	It is located in the CBD of the Nan'an District.	3 large climate-controlled indoor exhibition halls, electricity supply, wireless devices with web access, advanced ventilation system.
Chengdu International Conference & Exhibition Center	It is the largest exhibition center in the southwestern region of China, boasting an area of 230,000 square meters.	It is located in the Shawan Road, Chengdu.	It boasts the most well-equipped exhibition center in the southwest of China. Well-equipped exhibition halls, restaurants, bars, hotels, nightclubs, cinemas and supermarkets.
Kunming International Conference & Exhibition Center	It has an exhibition space of about 70,000 square meters.	It is located in No. 289 Chuncheng Road, Kunming.	Wireless and broadband Internet access, more than 2,000 sets of conference interpreting equipment, 2 large rear-projection LCD TVs.
Guiyang International Conference & Exhibition Center	With the total 976,300m^2 building area, Guiyang International Conference & Exhibition Center highlights the mountainous elements and ethnic group's cultural elements that are merely owned by Guizhou.	It is located in No.1 North Changling Road Guanshan Lake District, Guiyang.	Nearly 100 Integnated LCD/PDP/LED/Interactive Panels and other terminals are installed to provide omni-direstional information services in exhibition hall, coffee house, restaurant and other places. Electronic map, route index, cable TV, exhibition guide, etc. are utilized to realize highly-efficient and flexible information management and dispatching.

2．Role Play

[Situation A]

A visitor from the United States is inspecting on the basic facilities of an exhibition center. You are the guide of the center. You are asked to show him around.

Student A:　Foreign visitor

Student B:　Clerk of the exhibition center

[Sample dialogue]

A:　Hello, I'm David Johnson from the United States. I'm here to look for a suitable exhibition center for an upcoming exhibition in your city.

B:　Our exhibition center is the biggest and best one in this city. We have good facilities for exhibitions of different scales. Would you like to look around to get a general impression of it?

A:　Good, I'm willing to. Could you please show me around?

B:　My pleasure. When we go around the center, I'll make a general introduction of it.

A:　Oh, that's very kind of you.

B:　This exhibition center is the largest one in our city. It is made up of 2 kinds of exhibition space—indoor and outdoor. It covers an area of 30,000 square meters, perfect for an exhibition of large scale.

A: Would you please tell me the location of it? I hope it is very convenient for visitors to go to this place.

B: It is well-connected by public transportation. It is in the downtown area of …

A: What about its facilities?

B: …

[Direction] Try to have a conversation with your partner according to the following two situations. Practice your conversation until you can talk about the topic it freely to the class.

[Situation B]
Kunming International Conference and Exhibition Center.

[Situation C]
Chengdu International Conference and Exhibition Center.

Section Ⅲ Expansion Reading

[导读]

中国近年兴起了会展场所修建"热"。空间分布上，东部展览数远多于中部和西部，展览数量呈现从东部向西部逐渐递减的态势；全国有五大展览集中的区域。

Convention and Exhibition Centers in China

In recent years there has been a convention and exhibition center building boom in China. Many Chinese cities are building huge new C&E centers. The following are some famous ones among the many exhibition and conference centers in China.

The quantity of exhibitions in the eastern part of China is far larger than that in the west and central areas. Exhibitions concentrate on the following regions in China: Pearl River Delta, Yangtze River Delta, Bohai Rim, central China and western China. Pearl River Delta, Yangtze River Delta and Bohai Rim are the top 3 concentrated areas of both exhibitions and exhibition halls. Zhengzhou, Wuhan & Changsha are the top three cities in central China while Xi'an, Chongqing, Chengdu, Kunming compose another concentrated areas in the west.

China World Trade Center

China World Trade Center is a top market commercial mixed-use development center in China. Established in 1985 and fully functional in 1990, China World Trade Center has contributed significantly to the development of China's top-quality service industry and has facilitated the enhancement of investment environment in Beijing as well as foreign trade and economic cooperation. As the market leader in the industry, China World Trade Center has become a showcase for China's reform and opening, and is widely known as "The Place Where China Meets the World".

Shanghai New International Expo Center

The Shanghai New International Expo Center (SNIEC) is China's leading expo center, boasting state-of-the-art facilities. Situated in Shanghai's Pudong District, the heart of Chinese business, SNIEC has attracted worldwide attention since its opening in November, 2001. Featuring an easily accessible location, a pillar-free, single-story structure, and a wide array of expert on-site services, SNIEC has been experiencing rapid growth. It now hosts more than 60 world-class exhibitions each year and this number is set to grow in the near future.

Dalian Xinghai Convention & Exhibition Center

Dalian Xinghai Convention & Exhibition Center was established in 1996 and is a modern exhibition venue. It has luxurious halls that join multiple functions such as exhibition, conference, trade, information, catering and entertainment together. The center has state-of-the-art facilities, providing a full range of services. It also takes pride in its domestic top-class standard and has rich experience in the trade.

Qingdao International Convention Center

With an indoor exhibition area of 50,000 square meters, Qingdao International Convention Center (QICC) can hold 3,000 international standard exhibition booths. Its outdoor exhibition area reaches 80,000 square meters. It includes a luxurious conference room which can cater up to 400 persons, six meeting rooms (each has a capacity of 200 persons), and many negotiation rooms and VIP rooms. With a snack area of nearly 10,000 square meters, it supplies delicious food and beverage service.

Chinese Export Commodities Fair Exhibition Complexes

China Foreign Trade Center (CFTC) has become the official operator of Guangzhou International Convention & Exhibition Center. Presently, CFTC is running the two largest complexes in Guangzhou: the Pazhou Complex (namely the Guangzhou International Convention Exhibition Center) and Liuhua Complex of Chinese Export Commodities Fair. The total indoor exhibition area of the two complexes is up to 250,000 square meters.

1. Make the best choice according to the passage.

(1) In Central China, Zhengzhou, Wuhan and _____ are the most important exhibition regions.

  A. Nanning B. Chengdu C. Changsha D. Taiyuan

(2) The top 3 exhibition concentration areas in China are Pearl River Delta, Yangtze River Delta, and _____.

  A. Central China B. Western China C. Eastern China D. Bohai Rim

(3) A typical exhibition city in Pearl River Delta is _____.
　A．Shanghai　　　B．Nanning　　　C．Guangzhou　　　D．Hangzhou
(4) Which of the following exhibition centers is a joint venture of Chinese and western country companies?
　A．China World Trade Center.
　B．Dalian Xinghai Convention & Exhibition Center.
　C．Shanghai New International Expo Center.
　D．Chinese Export Commodities Fair Exhibition Complexes.
(5) Chinese Export Commodities Fair is held in _____ twice a year.
　A．Beijing　　　B．Shanghai　　　C．Guangzhou　　　D．Shenzhen
(6) There is a convention and exhibition center building boom in a lot of cities, esp. in _____.
　A．small towns　　　　　　　　B．county cities
　C．big cities　　　　　　　　　D．medium-sized cities
(7) The quantity of exhibitions is far _____ in the west and central China than that in the eastern part of China.
　A．bigger　　　B．smaller　　　C．remaining-stable　　　D．equal
(8) Which of the following centers is known as "The Place Where China Meets the World"?
　A．Chinese Export Commodities Fair Exhibition Complexes.
　B．China World Trade Center.
　C．Dalian Xinghai Convention & Exhibition Center.
　D．Shanghai New International Expo Center.

2. Translate the following sentences using as many language skills learned in this lesson as possible.
(1) 在空间分布上，中国东部展览数远多于中部和西部。
(2) 全国五大展览集中的区域是珠江三角洲、长江三角洲、渤海湾以及中部和西部。
(3) 位于北京的中国国际贸易中心是会展业的先驱，被誉为"中国与世界接轨的地方"。
(4) 大多数的会展中心都配备无线宽带上网、液晶电视。
(5) 上海新国际博览中心是上海浦东土地发展控股公司和德国三家全世界著名的会展公司合资修建的。

Section Ⅳ　The Internet Research

1. Which world-famous exhibition and conference centers have you ever heard of? Make a list of 4 such centers.

Name	Size	Location	Facilities
e.g. Dusseldorf, Germany	The exhibition complex is one of the largest in the world, covering nearly 2.5 million square feet of space.	Located in Dusseldorf, at River Rhaine.	17 climate-controlled halls, covered moving walkways, barber and beauty shops, restaurants, cafes, press clubs, banks, a post office, airline and train offices, etc.

续表

Name	Size	Location	Facilities

2. Research some information about the biggest exhibition centers in major south-west cities in China, such as Chengdu, Chongqing and Kunming. Make a chart to list the necessary information of location, size, facilities, transportation conveniences, convention types held, etc.

Section V　New Words You've Met in This Lesson

locate	vt.	坐落于……，使位于……
review	vt.	复习，温习
facility	n.	设施，设备
functional	adj.	有用的，能起作用的，产生影响的
contribute to	v.	有助于，促成
facilitate	vt.	使容易，促进，帮助
boast	vt.	有(引以为荣的事物)，夸耀；夸口
feature	vt.	以……为特色；给以显著地位
pillar-free	adj.	无柱(子)影响的；不受支柱妨碍的
luxurious	adj.	奢侈的；豪华的
snack	n.	小吃；点心；快餐
complex	n.	综合体，大型组合式建筑
commodity	n.	商品

Lesson 2

Space Size and Location
展台面积与位置

Section I　A Sample Dialogue

[Scene] Wang Lin, sales clerk with Kebo Exhibition is answering a phone call from an exhibit prospect who would like to get some information about reserving an exhibition booth.

Unit 2 Exhibition and Conference Centers in China 中国的会展中心

科博展览公司销售员王林接到了一个客户打来的电话。这位客户想要了解有关展位预订的信息。

Wang: Good afternoon. Kebo Exhibition Company. Can I help you?

Smith: Yes, please. I'm with Fillton in Turkey. I'd like to register for the 2008 International Auto Show in Sichuan.

Wang: May I have your name, sir?

Smith: I'm Levin Smith.

Wang: There are some booths available. If you send us your registration form and registration fees in two weeks' time, it is still possible for you to get one stand.

Smith: Can I register for it now on the phone?

Wang: Yes. What payment methods do you prefer?

Smith: By credit card, visa card.

Wang: OK. Would you mind answering me some questions to help sign up on the phone?

Smith: Not at all.

Wang: First, what is your company's current address? Phone number? E-mail?

Smith: It is at Flat 211, Building IV, 123 East Avenue, Fillton Town, Ankara, Turkey. The phone number is 25175-9011, and our e-mail address is *autoworld@filltonauto.com*. The company's name is Fillton Auto Assembling Corporation.

Wang: Yes, I got it. What kind of booth are you looking for, a standard package booth or a non-standard package booth?

Smith: I'm not sure. What do you charge?

Wang: The nine-square-meter booth costs ¥20,000 per unit while the six-square-meter booth is ¥15,000 per unit. Which do you prefer?

Smith: One nine-square-meter booth, please.

Wang: Sorry, sir, we cannot provide you with only one, because the minimum area for rent is 18 square meters. This exhibition specializes in auto products and auto parts, so the exhibitors usually need place at least this size.

Smith: 2 nine-square-meter booths cost ¥40,000, and 3 six-square-meter booths cost ¥45,000. Then I'll have 2 nine-square-meter booths.

Wang: OK. Where would you like your booths to be located?

Smith: Can I have two in the center?

Wang: Yes, you can. But I'd like to let you know that corner booths cost less than those in the center. They are open to two sides. And also they are close to exits and the traffic flow is almost the same as that in the center.

Smith: Thank you very much for informing me of this. It seems that we'd better have those corner booths.

Wang: OK, two nine-square-meter corner booths. May I have your credit card number?

Smith: It is 8600-18000-3021.

Wang: Thanks. I'll send you a letter to confirm your reservation soon. Anything else we can do for you?

Smith: I suppose not. Thank you. Goodbye.

Wang: Thanks for calling. Bye.

1. Read the conversation again and decide whether the following statements are true (T) or false(F).

(1) The company that Wang Lin is with is engaged in exhibition business. ( )

(2) Smith wants to take part in an auto show that is to be held soon. ( )

(3) Smith is signing up for the show on the phone. ( )

(4) Smith knows that the price of a booth depends on its location and size. ( )

(5) The traffic flow of the corner booths is the same as that in the center because they are close to the exits. ( )

(6) Smith cannot have a letter to prove that he has already booked the booths. ( )

(7) Smith will pay for the participation most likely by credit card. ( )

(8) Wang is very considerate to his customer. ( )

2. Discuss in groups.

Sum up what is needed to hold conferences/seminars. Suppose you are to hold an annual summary meeting. Please fill in the chart.

All applications for conference/seminar must be submitted to the organizer in a written form and pay the fee 7 days after confirmation. If you want to rent meeting rooms, please fill in the following checklist, then fax or e-mail it back to the organizer.

Classifications	Area /m^2	Number of people
NO.7 meeting room	105	80
NO.8 meeting room	120	100

Application date: _____   Using time: _____

Proposed speaker(s): _____   Position: _____

Company name(Chinese): _____

Proposed topic(Chinese): _____

Company name(English): _____

Proposed topic(English): _____

Country: _____

Brief synopsis (50 words at least):

_____

_____

_____

3. Match the jargons on the left with the Chinese equivalents on the right.

(1) booth number   a. 标准展位/台
(2) space application form   b. 付款方式
(3) service fee   c. 人流量
(4) bank account number   d. 最小起租面积
(5) minimum area for rent   e. 注册，登记
(6) closing date for application f. 展台号
(7) standard booth   g. 银行账号
(8) traffic flow   h. 报名截止日期
(9) payment method   i. 参展申请表
(10) register   j. 报名组织费

Section Ⅱ Communication Activities

1. Pair Work

The Costs of Different Booths

You are to rent a 3m×3m standard booth. Which kind do you prefer and why?

At a trade show, individual stands are classified into four categories: row stand, corner stand, end stand and island stand, with their costs different for the same area.

Prices for Stand Space

Stand Space (1 year contract 2009)

Row Stand(open on 1 side)	128 EURO/m^2
Corner Stand(open on 2 sides)	4 EURO/m^2
End Stand(open on 3 sides)	136 EURO/m^2
Island Stand(open on 4 sides)	140 EURO/m^2

2. Role Play

The following are price lists of two exhibition halls of a center. An exhibiting company is talking with a staff member in the center about the space rate.

Student A plays the role of a staff member in the center, and B is from an exhibiting company.

[Useful expressions] standard booth; specially-decorated booth; clear ground

会展中心招租费用表

方　　馆

展位规格		价　　格	位置及说明
标准展位	3m×3m	1,500 元/(个·展期)	二层
		1,200 元/(个·展期)	一层

续表

展位规格		价　　格	位置及说明
特殊展位	室内光地	140 元/(m² · 展期)	二层，36 m² 起租
		120 元/(m² · 展期)	一层，36 m² 起租
	室外空地	80 元/(m² · 展期)	室外广场，36 m² 起租
整租价格	室内展厅	9 元/(m² · 天)	二层，5,500 m² 整租
		7 元/(m² · 天)	一层，5,500 m² 整租

圆　馆

展位规格		价　　格	位置及说明
标准展位	3m×3m	1,300 元/(个 · 展期)	一层
		1,200 元/(个 · 展期)	二层
		1,050 元/(个 · 展期)	三层
特殊展位	室内光地	120 元/(m² · 展期)	一层，36 m² 起租
		100 元/(m² · 展期)	二层，36 m² 起租
	室外空地	80 元/(m² · 展期)	室外广场，36 m² 起租
	室外草坪	50 元/(m² · 展期)	室外草坪，一个建筑单位面积起租
整租价格	室内展厅	8 元/(m² · 天)	一层，3,800 m² 整租
		7 元/(m² · 天)	二层，2,500 m² 整租
		5 元/(m² · 天)	三层，1,800 m² 整租
	室外空地及草坪	4 元/(m² · 天)	室外广场，3,900m² 整租

[Sample dialogue]

A: Good morning. What can I do for you?

B: We are looking for a suitable venue to host an office facilities exhibition. We have made the initial research on the sites. Your center is one of our choices. I'd like to know more about the details, esp. the space costs.

A: We have two halls, one called Square Hall, and the other Circular Hall. The price varies.

B: What is your charge for a standard booth in the Square Hall? And what is the charge for renting the whole floor?

A: The price differs a little according to the floor. We ask for ￥1,500 for an indoor standard booth on the first floor and ￥1,200 on the second floor. If you rent the whole floor, the cost is ￥9 a square meter a day, and the floor is of 5,500 square meters.

B: Can there be any discount?

A: Yes. We can give you some discounts depending on the length of the show. If it lasts longer than 3 days, you can get a 5% off. If it is within 3 days, there is no favorable discount.

A: Thanks a lot.

B: You are welcome. If you need any further information, please contact us.

Section III Expansion Reading

[导读]

展会提供标准展位和室内外空场地等形式供参展商选择。同样的展位,针对不同来源的展商收费可能有差异。组展方会提供一些基本设备,如桌椅、电源插座等。但如需特殊服务(如上网、扩音器等),要事先说明,另行付费。

Size and Rent of Exhibition Space

Our exhibition center provides two kinds of exhibition space—the international standard exhibition booths and indoor and outdoor raw space. Exhibitor companies can make their choices according to the need of their business development.

The size of the standard exhibition booth is 3m×3m, which is equipped with an exhibition board with three facets, a company name board, one desk for consulting, two chairs, one fluorescent lamp and one socket. Please apply in advance if special services such as the Internet connection, loudspeakers, gas supplies are required. These services will be charged.

Standard Booths Rent Rate ($9m^2$)

A: Domestic exhibitors: ￥7,800 per booth.

B: Overseas exhibitors (including those from Hong Kong, Macau and Taiwan): $1,500 per booth.

Raw space is not equipped with any exhibition frames and facilities. Exhibitors can arrange the decoration work by themselves or entrust the decoration and construction company recommended by the organizer.

Raw Space Rent Rate

A (minimum area 36 square meters):

Domestic exhibitors: ￥780/m^2; Overseas exhibitors: $150/$m^2$.

B (minimum area 54 square meters):

Domestic exhibitors: ￥680/m^2; Overseas exhibitors: $120/$m^2$.

The procedure to sign up for the exhibition is as follows. After filling in the space application form, exhibitors need to mail or fax it to the organizing committee. Next they should remit the related payment to the appointed account number within ten days. Then they must fax the remitting return paper of bank to the organizing office in order to confirm application.

Water & Electricity Rental

The rental time is one exhibition period. Please look at the stylebook.

Item	Description	Unit	Unit Price (USD)	Notes
D01	Spotlight	1	17.00	
D02	Long arm spotlight	1	21.00	
D03	Track light	1	64.00	

续表

Item	Description	Unit	Unit Price (USD)	Notes
A01	Compressed air supply 3HP	1	972.00	
A02	DDD line(Refundable deposit for DDD $100.00)	1	515.00	without telephone set
A03	IDD line(Refundable deposit for IDD $580.00)	1	572.00	without telephone set
A04	Broadband	1	600.00	
A05	Water connector	1	786.00	

Notes

On-site rent: Rent fee will be subject to 100% surcharge. Unlisted items will be charged alone, all the leasehold items cannot be exchanged by the exhibitors.

No money will be returned if the exhibitor cancels the orders.

1. Read the passage again and decide whether the following statements are true (T) or false (F).

(1) The expense on raw space is similar to that on the standard booth of the same size. ( )

(2) Exhibitors can make choices from two kinds of exhibition space the exhibition center provides. ( )

(3) According to the current foreign exchange rate (1 dollar equals to ￥7 approximately), the overseas exhibitors pay more than ￥2,700 to rent a standard booth than the domestic ones. ( )

(4) Exhibitors cannot obtain special services, such as the Internet service, loudspeakers if they do not apply in advance. ( )

(5) The minimum area of raw space for rent is 36 square meters. ( )

(6) The rent expense of raw space of the same size is the same. ( )

(7) If the exhibitor does not order special services in advance, they will have to pay two times of the original rental price. ( )

(8) Item A02 is equipped with the telephone line which connects the whole country, while item A03 is telephone line that helps make international calls. ( )

2. Translate the following dialogues into English and practice it orally with a partner.

A：你好！我想报名参加城市园艺博览会。能电话报名吗？

B：可以。不过，要等到你把注册费汇款进账后才能予以展位确认。

A：好的。请为我预订一个标准展位。

B：你要底楼展位还是二楼展位？

A：是不是位置不同，价格也不一样呢？

B：底楼位置好，当然就贵些。不过二楼以上展位可免收两平方米的展位费。

A：那就订二楼吧。

B：没问题。一个二楼标准展位的费用是12,000元。

Section Ⅳ The Internet Research

1. What is the regular space rent of Chongqing International Convention and Exhibition

Center located in Nanping District?

2. When is the "in" season and "out" season of the exhibition industry? Is there any difference in space rate?

3. There are quite a few exhibition centers in Chengdu, as well as in other medium-size and large-size cities. Does the space rent that the centers in the same city offer vary a lot, or slightly? Can you give some reasons for this phenomenon?

Section V New Words You've Met in This Lesson

assemble	vi.	装配，组装
specialize (in)	vi.	专攻，专门从事
raw space	n.	展览空地
facet	n.	(事物的)面，方面
board	n.	板，牌子，纸板，木板
consult	v.	请教，咨询
fluorescent	adj.	荧光的，发荧光的
socket	n.	插孔；插座
frame	n.	骨架，构架，框架
entrust	v.	委托，托付
minimum	adj.	最小的
organizing committee	n.	组织委员会
appointed	adj.	指定的，约定的
confirm	v.	肯定，确认
stylebook	n.	样本
compressed air supply 3HP	n.	中央空压器 3 匹
IDD line	n.	国际直拨电话
remit	vt.	汇款
return paper	n.	回执单
water connector	n.	给排水
surcharge	n.	加收费

Section VI Writing Related to EC Industry

Read and complete the chart.

Space Application Form
(展位申请表)

Company _____	Contact Person _____
Address_____	Zip _____
Tel. _____	Fax. _____

续表

Company _____		Contact Person _____	
E-mail _____		Website _____	
Please tick and fill in the blanks where appropriate.			
Option	Unit(s) square meter required × Unit cost = Total cost		
Package stand 9 m^2/Unit	￥2,500/Unit(s)		
Package stand 6 m^2/Unit	￥1,700/Unit(s)		
Attendance	A: ￥1,800 per person B: ￥2,800 per person	A: B:	Total ￥_____
Incidental expense	￥3,000 per person		Total ￥_____
Service fee	￥3,000/Unit	_____ Unit(s)	Total ￥_____

Total _____
Signature _____
Date _____
Note: There is a minimum area of 36 m^2 for raw space

Section Ⅶ Review of This Unit

1. Jargons in This Unit

domestic & overseas exhibitors	国内和国外参展商
standard booth	标准展位/台
incentive tour	奖励旅游
cultural events	文化事件/活动
space application form	参展申请表
registration form	登记表
booth personnel	展台工作人员
minimum area for rent	起租面积
state-of-the-art facilities	一流的/最先进的设施
nation-wide meeting	国家级会议/全国会议
exhibition facilities/venues	展览设施/场地
outdoor /indoor space	室外/室内展场
package booth	一揽子收费展台
payment method	付款方式

2. Sentence Patterns/Practical Dialogues

(1) In a narrow sense,…only refers to…

(2) They specialize in…respectively.

(3) Would you like to walk around to get a general impression of …?

(4) … is well-connected by public transportation.

(5) Can I register for … now on the phone?

(6) Each standard package booth costs at least ￥20,000 and non-standard package booth at least ￥15,000.

(7) I'd like to let you know that…

3. Writing Related to EC Industry

Fill out an application form.

Unit 3

Preparations for the Exhibition
会 展 筹 备

单元目标

1. 了解中国知名展览会。
2. 理解参展方和组展方的不同立场和不同筹备工作。
3. 领会主题的确定是展览会的首要环节，根据具体案例制定不同的展览会主题。
4. 学会在展会中进行自我介绍及介绍他人。
5. 掌握邀请信的写法。

Lesson 1

Preparations by the Host
组展方的准备工作

Section Ⅰ A Sample Dialogue

[Scene] Mr. Green, the service manager of the Organizing Committee for the International Automobile Exhibition, is talking with his secretary, Mary, about the preparations for the coming exhibition.

国际汽车博览会组委会的服务部经理格林先生与秘书玛丽正在谈论展会开幕前的准备情况。

Mr. Green: That's all for today's meeting. Mary, please stay for a few more minutes.

Mary: OK.

Mr. Green: Mary, I want to know about the preparations in detail. How are you getting along with the final check-up?

Mary: I've contacted each keynoter personally about the meeting schedule.

Mr. Green: Did you ask them about their specific requirements?

Mary: Yes, all of them will use slides and the overhead projector.

Mr. Green: You should personally check them to make sure the slides and the projector are working properly.

Mary: I have checked them. There were a few black spots on the slides, but they've been cleaned.

Mr. Green: Don't forget about the audio aids. How about the microphones and loudspeakers? They said they would like cordless microphones.

Mary: I have got them ready, sir.

Mr. Green: Good. Have you prepared some paper and pencils for the attendants?

Mary: Yes, of course. All the writing materials needed are included in the meeting folders, which are placed on the table at the entrance to the meeting hall.

Mr. Green: Have you told the reception desk that several hostesses are needed to usher the delegates.

Mary: Yes, sir. I have also prepared the signs needed in specific locations.

Mr. Green: Excellent. We don't want any problem. We should always live up to our promises, you know?

Mary:	I know. Such an important event could easily be harmed by even the smallest mistake.
Mr. Green:	You are right. You'd better double-check, just to be sure.
Mary:	OK. Later I'll report back to you about my final check-up and let you know that everything is going perfect on the checklist.
Mr. Green:	Fine. Well, have you taken down the notes about the planner's latest changes and requests? You must have them typed up and added to the documents.
Mary:	OK, I'll also inform the department heads of those changes and requests.
Mr. Green:	That's good. Thank you!
Mary:	You're welcome, sir!

1. Read the conversation again and decide whether the following statements are true (T) or false (F).

(1) Mr. Green runs into Mary and they have a talk about the meeting planning.　　(　)

(2) Mary has informed the reception desk that several hostesses(迎宾小姐) are needed.
　　　　　　　　　　　　　　　　　　　　　　　　　　　　　　　　　　　(　)

(3) Mary says she has contacted each meeting speaker and made proper arrangements for him or her.　　(　)

(4) Mr. Green tells Mary that the meeting group needs several microphones on the table.　(　)

(5) Paper and pencils will be prepared in the drawers of the desks.　　(　)

(6) Mr. Green thinks the convention center should maintain its good image among customers by doing what it has promised.　　(　)

(7) There was no problem with the slides and overhead projector right from the beginning.　　(　)

(8) The meeting planner adds or cuts off some detailed activities to and from the specification sheet.　　(　)

2. Act as Mr. Green and your partner as Mary to discuss the preparations of the following items. Then switch the roles.

VIP pin	Sign	Nameplate	Plastron(胸花)

3. Match the jargons on the left with the Chinese equivalents on the right.

(1) usher　　　　　　　　　　　　a. 主要发言人

(2) cordless microphone　　　　　　b. 投影仪

(3) projector　　　　　　　　　　 c. 文件夹

(4) double-check   d. 幻灯片
(5) folder   e. 无线话筒
(6) slide   f. 引座，引领
(7) keynoter   g. 核实
(8) microphone   h. 时刻表
(9) reception desk   i. 话筒
(10) schedule   j. 接待处

Section II Communication Activities

1. Pair Work

Practice the introductory dialogues with your partners.

[Sample dialogue]

A: My name is Wang Tong, convention service secretary.

B: Nice to meet you. My name is Li Fang, from China Technical Research Center. Here is my business card.

A: Nice to meet you, too. Here is my business card. I am in charge of the secretarial duties of this convention. If you have any problem, please don't hesitate to contact me.

B: It is the first time for me to attend such an exhibition. I guess I will trouble you a lot.

A: It's my pleasure to assist you. By the way, have you ever been to this city?

B: No, it's my first time.

A: Tonight local musical instruments will be played in a concert. You may go there and experience the local music style.

B: That's fabulous! I have no plans for tonight. When and where?

A: You can check it in the pamphlet. There are more shows this week. You can't miss them!

B: That would be wonderful. Thank you so much!

A: You're welcome.

[Situation]

A			B		
Name	Company	Position	Name	Company	Position
Liu Jialing	Austin Advertising Agency	Marketing Manager	Andy Lee	Great Universal Store	General Manager
Peter Johnson	Tropic Air Services	Sales Representative	William Bush	Atlantic Container Line	Sales Manager
Wang Jia	Dongsheng Clothes Import & Export Corporation	Senior Secretary	Jiang Ting	Unique Chemicals Import & Export Corporation	Producing Manager

续表

A			B		
Name	Company	Position	Name	Company	Position
Freeman Wharton	Shell Oil Company	Senior Salesman	Zhang Jing	Shanghai Textiles Import & Export Corporation	Deputy Sales Manager

2. Role Play

To introduce others to new friends.

[Sample dialogue]

Mr. Wales: John, let me introduce Mr. Lee from Shell Oil Company to you.

Mr. Hilton: How do you do? Mr. Lee, I am John Hilton from China Mobile.

Mr. Lee: How do you do? Mr. Hilton.

Mr. Wales: Mr. Lee has recently been promoted to be the Branch Manager of Shell Oil in our city.

Mr. Hilton: Congratulations! Shell Oil has a good reputation here.

Mr. Lee: I hope it can be even better in the near future.

Mr. Hilton: That's for sure.

Mr. Wales: I believe so! Let's toast to Shell! *(Holding up the glass.)*

Mr. Lee: To Shell! *(Holding up the glass.)*

Mr. Hilton: To Shell! *(Holding up the glass.)*

[Situations]

Suppose you were Shirley. Introduce the other three people who do not know each other at all, so that they can talk about the coming fair.

(1) Shirley, the secretary of the organizing committee of a fair.

(2) Mr. Wharton from General Motors.

(3) John Hilton representing the ABC Appliances Company in China.

(4) Ms. Berry from China Youth Travel Agency.

Additional Information:

1) Reaffirming Commitments

(1) I assure you that we can provide you with the best meeting.

(2) Everything is perfectly ready for the opening ceremony of the exhibition.

(3) A good beginning is half the success.

(4) We can ensure a totally successful meeting.

(5) We have a good reputation of living up to our promises, and our service is the best.

(6) You can rest assured that our staff will strictly fulfill their duties found in the function sheet.

(7) We are confident that there will be no embarrassing mistakes with the conference.

2) Revising Convention Program

(1) Ten of our delegates won't be able to come for the meeting. So can you make changes in the room arrangement?

(2) Is it possible for us to use the overhead projector?

(3) There are not enough plastrons for all the VIPs, so more plastrons should be taken to the exhibition center immediately.

(4) One of the keynoters cannot arrive until tomorrow afternoon, so the agenda should be changed accordingly.

(5) Sunday afternoon's meeting won't end until 6 o'clock. Can you put off the meal time to 6: 30 pm.?

Section Ⅲ Expansion Reading

▶[导读]

第 10 届中国国际展览和会议展示会于 2009 年 1 月在南京国际展览中心举行,展会主题为: 对话、交流、和谐、进步。

The 10th China International Trade Show for Exhibition and Conference Industry

Date: January 14-16, 2009.

Place: Nanjing International Exhibition Center.

Sponsors:

China Council for the Promotion of International Trade (CCPIT);

The Global Association of the Exhibition Industry (UFI);

International Association of Exhibitions and Events (IAEE);

Society of Independent Show Organizers(SISO).

Organizer:

China Association for Exhibition Centers;

China International Exhibition Center Group Corporation.

Co-organizers:

Nanjing Conference Exhibition Office;

Nanjing International Exhibition Center;

CAEC Professional Committee for Exhibition Organization;

CAEC Professional Committee for Exhibition Engineering;

CAEC Professional Committee for Exhibition Theory Research.

Supported by:

Jiangsu Easthigh Convention & Exhibition Group Co., Ltd;

Jiangsu Provincial Convention & Exhibition Industry Association.

Theme: Dialogue, Communication, Harmony, Development.

Exhibition Aim:

Nanjing, a historic and civilized city, is an important industrial production base. It is an important center of transportation and communication in the eastern region of China, and a national base of superior education and scientific research as well. All of these make the Nanjing Exhibition an increasingly progressing and greatly supported industry.

The aim of InterExpo 2009 is to speed up the development of China's Exhibition Industry and promote exchange and fair competition within the industry. InterExpo 2009 bases itself upon the market. It focuses on high quality and continues to operate in a professional mode to serve as an exchange and cooperative stage for companies at home and abroad to improve their images. It strives to establish and maintain good relations with customers.

As an important event of the China Expo Forum for International Cooperation (CEFCO 2009), the Global Association of the Exhibition Industry (UFI), the International Association of Exhibitions and Events (IAEE) and the Society of Independent Show Organizers (SISO), will hold the 10th China International Trade Show for Exhibition and Conference Industry (InterExpo 2009) at the Nanjing International Exhibition Center on January 14-16, 2009. This will be jointly organized by China Council for the Promotion of International Trade. Show organizers, booth contractors, service suppliers, government bodies, exhibition media, etc., will once again gather together in Nanjing for the grand gathering of the convention and exhibition industry.

CAEC sincerely extends the invitation to you to participate in InterExpo 2009.

Exhibitor Categories:

(1) Trade show and conference organizers, exhibition companies.

(2) Exhibition and conference facilities, exhibition complex, convention centers, resorts.

(3) Designers and contractors.

(4) Equipment suppliers of display material and accessories.

(5) Exhibition freight forwarders.

(6) IT product and service, e-business service.

(7) Associations of commerce, trade promotion organizations.

(8) Governmental convention management bodies.

(9) Business travel agencies, hotels, airlines.

(10) Trade show media, magazines and web companies.

(11) Service suppliers related to trade show.

General Information:

(1) Moving in: January 11-13, 2009.

(2) Exhibition: January 14-16, 2009.

(3) Moving out: January 16, 2009 (after 14:00).

1. Answer the following questions orally according to the passage.

(1) What is the full name of InterExpo 2009?

(2) Where is InterExpo 2009 held?

(3) Who are the sponsors?

(4) Who are the organizers?

(5) What is the theme of the InterExpo 2009?

(6) What is the exhibition aim of InterExpo 2009?

(7) How long does the convention last?

(8) What does InterExpo 2009 exhibit?

2. Translate the following sentences using as many language skills learned in this lesson as possible.

(1) 主办单位。

(2) 承办单位。

(3) 协办单位。

(4) 你不仅可以在网上查到这次展会的主题和宗旨，还可以在网上预订展位。

(5) 这次展览会将展出全世界最新的IT产品，并且召开关于IT行业发展的研讨会。

(6) 展会的主题最终确定为城市、发展、和谐。

(7) 这次展会的进场日期和撤展日期已经确定，并已通过手机短信告知所有参展商。

Section Ⅳ The Internet Research

1. Visit the website (http://www.tdctrade.com) and find out an exhibition of your interest.

2. Take down the following information about the exhibition.

(1) Name of the exhibition.

(2) Time, Place, Theme, Aims.

(3) Categories of exhibits.

(4) Types of entry.

(5) Which trade is it in?

(6) Features & advantages.

(7) History (past successes).

3. Work with your partners to create one convention. Design the following details: date, place, theme, objective, sponsors, organizers and co-organizers.

Section V New Words You've Met in This Lesson

delegate	n.	代表
plastron	n.	胸花
secretarial	adj.	秘书的
fabulous	adj.	极好的
pamphlet	n.	小册子
textile	n.	纺织品
reputation	n.	名声
sponsor	n.	主办方
supplier	n.	供应商
freight	n.	货物
municipal	adj.	市政的
aeronautics	n.	航空学
administration	n.	局
confer	v.	协商
harmonious	adj.	和谐的

Section VI Writing Related to EC Industry

Write an invitation letter on behalf of the Organizing Committee of the 10th China International Trade Show for Exhibition and Conference Industry. For more information please refer back to the expansion reading material in this lesson. A sample letter is given below.

An Invitation Letter

June 8, 2009

Dear Sir or Madam:

"China General Aviation Convention 2009" will be held from October 26-27 in Xi'an, China, with the great support of the Municipal Government of Xi'an, Shaanxi Province of China, China Aviation Industrial Base, and Chinese Society of Aeronautics.

With great support of Xi'an municipal government, Union Civil Aviation North-west Administration and other local departments, warmly invite people from home and abroad, those inside and outside of the industry, leading authorities and VIPs in multiple fields, as well as investors who have the intention to take part in the development of general aviation, to attend this "China General Aviation Convention 2009." We invite you to explore jointly the policies related to Chinese general aviation market and the investment environment, the bottleneck of general aviation policies, and local government's planning for promoting general aviation development.

We also invite you to discuss all the pressing issues, and make joined efforts in developing the largest and "virgin land" market of general aviation in the world.

This convention will be a festival for the investors. Hundreds of Chinese and foreign experts, entrepreneurs and government leaders gather in Xi'an to confer on the development measures of Chinese general aviation industry, to jointly create the harmonious atmosphere of cooperation, and to share the general aviation industry policies, historical opportunity and the challenge of market. Glory and dream belong to those wise and courageous investors and collaborators of general aviation industry.

Time: October 26-27, 2009

Venue: Xifei Hotel, Yanliang, Xi'an China (China Aviation Industrial Base)

Application Due Date: October.10, 2009

Website of the Convention: http://ga.caib.gov.cn.

Yours sincerely,
Organizing Committee of
China General Aviation Convention 2009

Lesson 2

Preparations by the Exhibitors
参展方的准备工作

Section I A Sample Dialogue

[Scene] Two people working in an import and export company are chatting about the World Expo 2010 in China.

一家进出口公司的两名员工正讨论2010年上海世界博览会的情况。

Jack: Betty, do you know about the World Expo 2010?

Betty: Yes, I know it from the news in *China Daily*. The festival will be held in Shanghai in 2010. Do you know more about that?

Jack: World Expositions are shows of human inspirations and thoughts.

Betty: Could you give me more details about this?

Jack: Yes, of course. Since 1851, the World Exposition has gained greater fame as a grand event for economic, scientific, technological and cultural exchanges. It serves as an important platform for displaying historical experience, exchanging creative ideas, and looking to the future.

Betty: What are the highlights of the World Expo 2010 in China?

Jack: Expo 2010 Shanghai China will be the first World Exposition in a developing country. It will be a great event to explore urban life in the 21st century. 55% of the world population is expected to live in cities by the year 2010. The future urban life will be a subject of global interest.

Betty: Oh, I see. So, "City" is the theme of the exposition?

Jack: You're right. The theme is "Better City, Better Life".

Betty: The exhibitors can't be individuals but countries or cities. Is that so?

Jack: Yes, you are right. About 200 countries or cities will participate in this exposition. But about 70 million visitors will be expected to come.

Betty: Oh, by the way, what is this?

Jack: This is the mascot created from a Chinese character meaning people; the mascot "Haibao" embodies the character of Chinese culture.

Betty: How cute it is! How about this emblem?

Jack: The emblem, showing the image of three people—you, me, him/her holding hands together, symbolizes the big family of mankind.

Betty: When will the exhibition be held?

Jack: From May 1 to October 31, 2010.

Betty: That's a long time.

Jack: I believe Chinese people will present to the world a successful, and unforgettable exposition.

Betty: I think so!

1. Answer the following questions orally according to the dialogue.

(1) How does Betty know about World Expo at the beginning?

(2) What does World Expo display to the world people?

(3) What is the main feature of World Expo 2010 in China?

(4) Why does World Expo 2010 focus on city life?

(5) How many participants will join in the exposition?

(6) What is the name of the mascot of World Expo 2010? What does it symbolize?

(7) What does the emblem of World Expo 2010 demonstrate?

(8) When will World Expo 2010 be held?

Unit 3　Preparations for the Exhibition 会展筹备

2. Try to talk about 13th Shanghai International Automobile Industry Exhibition in pairs using the information below.

Items	Content	Remarks
Name	13th Shanghai International Automobile Industry Exhibition	Short form: Auto Shanghai 2009
Date	April 22-28, 2009	Media Day: April 20-21, 2009
Venue	Shanghai New International Expo Center	
Theme	Art of Innovation	Global climate changing; New energy; Energy saving and emission(排放) reduction.
Exhibitors	International giants: GM, Ford, Chrysler, Benz, BMW, Toyota, Honda, Nissan, Volkswagen, Audi, Skoda, Citroen, Renault, Peugeot, Volvo, Mazda, Hyundai, Kia. Luxury cars: Porsche, Ferrari, Maserati, Lamborghini, Maybach, Bentley, Spyker. Domestic cars: FAW, SAIC, Dongfeng, Chang'an, GAC, BAW, BYD, Haima, Great Wall Auto, Brilliance, Changfeng, Greeley, Jianghuai, Hafei.	
Official Website	http://www.autoshanghai.org	
Total Area	Over 170,000 square meters	
Visitors	Over 600,000	

3. Match the jargons on the left with the Chinese equivalents on the right.

(1) cocktail party　　　　　　　a. 会议议程
(2) sign　　　　　　　　　　　　b. 会议明细表
(3) convention agenda　　　　　c. 路标
(4) arrival pattern　　　　　　　d. 代表铭牌
(5) VIP pin　　　　　　　　　　e. 鸡尾酒会
(6) nameplate　　　　　　　　　f. 操作清单
(7) specification sheet　　　　　g. 总结会
(8) function sheet　　　　　　　h. 会前会
(9) pre-convention meeting　　　i. 贵宾徽章
(10) post-convention meeting　　j. 抵店方式

Section Ⅱ　Communication Activities

1. Pair Work

Introduce the Canton Fair to a person who knows little about that.

[Sample dialogue]

A: Do you know about the Canton Fair?

B: Not much. What does it show?

A: All kinds of commodities. The fair mainly features export trade, though import business is also done here.

B: Is it a fair for export companies in Guangdong Province?

A: No, it is the largest trade fair in China with companies from all parts of China.

B: When is it held?

A: It is held in the spring and autumn seasons of each year.

[Situations]

Here is more information about the Canton Fair. Continue the dialogue with your partner.

Background Information about the Canton Fair

The Canton Fair has been recognized as "China's No.1 Fair" for several reasons. First of all, it has the longest history, dating back to 1957. It is also acclaimed to have the highest level of export commodities fair, the largest scale of visitors, as well as the most complete exhibit variety. Furthermore, the Canton Fair is recognized as having the largest buyer attendance, the broadest buyer distribution, the best business turnover rate (周转率), and the best credit standing in China. Its full name prior to 2007 was the Chinese Export Commodities Fair (中国出口商品交易会), but was renamed the China Import and Export Fair (中国进出口商品交易会) in 2007.

The Fair is held in Guangzhou in both the spring and the autumn. Forty-eight Trading Delegations, composed of thousands of China's best foreign trade corporations with good credibility and sound financial capabilities take part in the Fair. These include foreign trade companies, factories, scientific research institutions, foreign invested enterprises, wholly foreign-owned enterprises, private enterprises, etc..

Besides the traditional way of negotiating face to face, the Fair holds the Canton Fair online. The Fair mainly features export trade, although import business is also done here. Apart from the above-mentioned, various types of business activities such as economic and technical cooperation and exchanges, commodity inspection, insurance, transportation, advertising, consultation, etc. are also carried out in flexible ways. Business people from all over the world are gathering in Guangzhou, exchanging business information and developing friendships.

2. Role Play

[Sample dialogue]

Chen Lu, a staff member of China Export Commodities Fair, is talking with Mike Miller, a foreign business man at the entrance of the fair.

Chen Lu: Look! The dragon dance begins over there!

Mike Miller: Is this the traditional Chinese celebration for an opening ceremony?

Chen Lu: Yes, Chinese people play dragon dance on important occasions, like the Spring Festival. So you see the Export Commodities Fair is also a great event in China.

Unit 3 Preparations for the Exhibition 会展筹备

Mike Miller: I've heard it's held twice a year.
Chen Lu: Yes. It's held biannually in Guangzhou—the Spring Fair and the Autumn Fair. Through the Fair, China can pursue more foreign trade.
Mike Miller: I'm sure friends in business circles of various countries will participate in the Fair.
Chen Lu: Right. It's really a sea of people. The businessperson are invited for discussions on import and export issues. So the Fair promotes friendship as well as business.
Mike Miller: This is my first time to the Fair. Let's have a look right now.
Chen Lu: All right.

[Situations]

(1) Chen Lu is showing Mike Miller around in the autumn fair of the Canton Fair in 2008. Mike Miller wants to see some traditional Chinese commodities. Chen introduces tea, silk and spirits to him.

(2) Chen Lu and Mike Miller are chatting about the importance and great potential of the Canton Fair.

(3) Chen Lu and Mike Miller are chatting about the pamphlet on this year's spring fair. Mike Miller wants to find a supplier of kids' clothes in China.

(4) Chen Lu and Mike Miller are chatting on phone. Mike decides to book a booth for the upcoming spring fair.

Three Phases of the Spring Fair in 2009

Phase I (April 15-19, 2009)	Phase II (April 24-28, 2009)	Phase III (May 3-7, 2009)
Large Machinery and Equipment,	Kitchenware & Tableware,	Men and Women's Clothes,
Small Machinery,	General Ceramics,	Kids' Wear,
Bicycles,	Art Ceramics,	Underwear,
Motorcycles,	Home Decorations,	Sports and Casual Wear,
Chemical Products,	Furniture,	Furs,
Hardware,	Weaving,	Leather,
Tools,	Iron Arts,	Home Textiles,
Vehicles,	Gardening Products,	Textile,
Construction Machinery,	Stone and Iron Products,	Carpets,
Household Appliances,	Household Items,	Food,
Computers,	Personal Care Products,	Medicines and Health Products,
Lighting Equipment,	Toiletries,	Sports,
Building materials,	Clocks,	Travel and Recreation Products,
Sanitary and Bathroom Equipment.	Watches,	Office Supplies,
	Instruments,	Shoes,
	Toys,	Cases and Bags,
	Gifts,	Medical Devices.
	Festival Products.	

Section Ⅲ Expansion Reading

[导读]

要在展会中获益，参展方的准备活动是至关重要的环节。其中不可忽视的有选择适合的展会、有针对性地准备展品、挑选参会人员。

Exhibition Preparation Advice

Choose the Right Exhibition

Look at the shows available for your industry and the exhibitions in the industries of your target markets. Investigate the exhibitor lists to see who else will be there and look at the number of visitors and research from the previous year's show. Ask for details of the marketing plan for the exhibition—who will be targeted, how and how many, especially if the show is in its first year.

Supported by good marketing, exhibitions in their first year can be hidden treasure, as visitors may attend just to see what it's all about—particularly if the organizer is offering a good incentive to attend, such as a top keynote speaker or free coffee vouchers!

Prepare Your Display Items

If you thought choosing and booking a show was the difficult bit, you'd be wrong! Once the show is booked, the hard work really starts!

How can you best display your company in a way that fits the target audience of this exhibition? Why should they buy from you? What should they buy from you? How can you maximize your returns?

The first important step is the design of your exhibition stand—don't over-complicate things. Visitors should be able to see in three seconds who you are, what you do and one reason to buy from you. If it takes longer, you've lost them. Visitors on average visit only ten stands at an exhibition, so how do you ensure they visit yours?

Visitors make first decisions about companies through non-verbal messages, such as the size and design of the stand. It is very similar to meeting a person for the very first time—you don't get a second chance to make a first impression, and minds are made up within the first three seconds, primarily based on visual effect.

Exhibitions have a hidden weapon, however, they are the only marketing medium that can appeal to all the senses at once—count the coffee machines next time you visit and you will begin to understand the power this can offer the exhibitor. Sounds, pleasant smells and experiences can all add to the visitor experience at an exhibition—and we all remember the stands with carpets and massage cushions—so be sure to include some of these in your preparation.

It's also important not to block the front of your stand—visitors who are interested in your products will let you know by stepping into your stand space. It's similar to walk through a shop door. If there's something blocking the front of your display, you're stopping people qualifying their interest in your product / service—and making it much harder for your team.

Choose the Right Staff

Exhibitions are an unnatural environment for sales creatures—the sales message must be shortened for the audience and many visitors must be addressed in a short space of time. For this reason, sales people are very important at an exhibition.

Visitors attend exhibitions to find out about new things and search for information. Technical staff on hand would be able to answer these questions, while sales staff maybe cannot. In addition, technical staff may find new product ideas and developments through conversations at exhibitions.

Research and customer feedback are key to any company's future success. Can owner/managers afford not to attend an exhibition and keep track of their industry?

1. Read the passage again and decide whether the following statements are true (T) or false(F).

(1) When preparing an exhibition, you need just consider the shows that are available for your industry. ( )

(2) Exhibitor lists, visitor numbers and research from the previous year's show can demonstrate the level of an exhibition. ( )

(3) Exhibitors should be especially cautious if the show is in its first year. ( )

(4) Choosing and booking a show is just the beginning of taking part in an exhibition with more challenges to come. ( )

(5) Over-complicate things should be avoided in the design of a stand for a trade show. ( )

(6) It is very useful to block visitors, as they will have more opportunities to introduce the products face-to-face. ( )

(7) Sales people, technical staff and even managers should attend an exhibition. ( )

(8) Research and customer feedback are key to any company's future success. ( )

2. Translate the following sentences using as many language skills learned in this lesson as possible.

(1) 参展商、参会人数和上届展会的情况都能说明一个展会的水平。

(2) 这个全球最大的服装贸易会，每年9月8—11日在美国纽约举办。

(3) 中国出口商品交易会以突出中国传统文化和现代化为主要特色。

(4) 一次成功的会展不仅能够吸引国内和国外的商家来参展，而且能够盈利。

(5) 技术人员能够回答销售人员不能回答的问题。

Section Ⅳ The Internet Research

1. Research on the Internet after class to look for information about at least 3 important trade fairs in China in recent three years.

2. Suppose you are working for an automobile company. What kind of trade fairs might be your choice? Name three of these fairs.

Section V New Words You've Met in This Lesson

inspiration	n.	鼓舞，灵感
mascot	n.	吉祥物
embody	vt.	体现
emblem	n.	徽章
symbolize	vt.	象征
credibility	n.	可信性
consultation	n.	咨询
upcoming	adj.	即将到来的
toiletry	n.	卫浴设备
sanitary	adj.	卫生的
recreation	n.	娱乐
incentive	n.	刺激，诱因
voucher	n.	凭证
massage	n.	按摩
cushion	n.	垫子
track	n.	踪迹，痕迹，足迹

Section VI Review of This Unit

1. Jargons in This Unit

usher	引座，引领
cordless microphone	无线话筒
projector	投影仪
double-check	核实
cocktail party	鸡尾酒会
pre-convention meeting	会前会
post-convention meeting	总结会
function sheet	会议明细表
nameplate	代表铭牌
VIP pin	贵宾徽章

续表

plastron	胸花
arrival pattern	抵店方式
specification sheet	操作清单

2. Sentence Patterns/Practical Dialogues

1) Self-introduction

(1) My name is …I am in charge of …duties.

(2) Let me introduce myself. I'm …, the manager of… I am responsible for...

(3) Allow me to introduce myself. My name is ... Please call me …

(4) Good morning. My name is …, from China. This is my business card.

2) Introducing others

(1) Gentleman, let me introduce … to you.

(2) How do you do?

(3) Ladies and gentlemen, this is … from ... (company)

(4) Glad to meet you.

(5) I'd like you all to meet... He/ She represents …Company.

(6) Pleased to meet you, Mr...

(7) I'm honored to introduce to you Mr… from… Company.

(8) We are delighted to meet you.

3. Writing Related to EC Industry

Write an invitation letter on behalf of the organizing committee of a fair.

Unit 4

Participation in an Exhibition
参 展

单元目标

1. 了解展台设计策划的实施步骤。
2. 了解展览设计中所涉及的方方面面之间的关系,尤其是展览设计师与客户的关系。
3. 学习处理展会期间可能发生的各种问题,如展品推介及突发情况处理。
4. 学会收集资料,能够编写简单的英文产品宣传材料。

Lesson 1

Decorating: Stand Construction and Reception
布展：展台搭建和接待

> **Section Ⅰ A Sample Dialogue**

[Scene] In 2009, the First China West Tour Industry Exposition has been held in the Chongqing International Convention and Exhibition Center. In order to perfect the booth construction, the Municipal Bureau of Tourism of Chongqing, organizer of the exposition, was going to hold a public bidding for the official show contractor of the exposition. The New World Exhibition Services assigned Li Li, the Show Manager, to get some information about the exposition.

"第一届中国西部旅游产业博览会"（简称"西博会"）于 2009 年在重庆国际会展中心举行。为了更好地推介西部旅游产品，重庆市旅游局对会展承建商进行了招标。新世界会展服务公司派出其展览管理经理李立前去了解情况。

Li Li: Hi, Mr. Huang. I am Li Li from the New World Exhibition Services. I am here to collect some information about the upcoming exposition in Chongqing.

Information desk: How may I assist you?

Li Li: Our company is very interested in the public bidding for the official contractor of the First China West Tour Industry Exposition. I would like to know what the basic requirements are for the official show contractor.

Information desk: Well, there are some requirements. First, as the official show contractor, it must be capable of constructing all the booths in a proper way, that is to say, in a way that will cater to the needs of the exhibitors. Second, apart from stand construction, the company providing the service is expected to prepare for the reception of exposition visitors. Last but not the least, the Municipal Tourism Bureau will examine the qualifications of the companies engaged in the bidding. Financial status, relating working experiences in this field, and competences of its staff will all be considered.

Li Li: That sounds quite reasonable. I am very confident that our company is a strong competitor in this bidding. By the way, how can I, on behalf of our company, apply for the bidding?

Information desk: It is quite easy. Here is the application form. Please fill out the form as directed. After that, please return the form to the information desk. We will contact you as soon as possible.

Li Li: That's good! Thank you very much!

(An exhibitor from Xi'an of the Shaanxi Province goes to the Information Desk to ask about the stand construction and reception of visitors.)

Exhibitor: Hi, I am from Xi'an. I am here for some information.

Information desk: Yes, what can I do for you?

Exhibitor: As this exposition is the first one in tour industry in western China, we take it very seriously. In order to attract more visitors to our booth, we want to build a unique stand. Is it possible for us to employ our own contractor?

Information desk: I'm afraid that is not possible. There is only one contractor officially recognized by the organizer of this exposition. If you have any requirements for your booth, you can talk to the contractor.

Exhibitor: It is a pity that we can't hire our own contractor.

Information desk: We hope you can understand this arrangement. It will be much easier for the organizer to use a standard stand construction, and to protect the exhibition hall from any damage. Actually the official show contractor is very capable and is able to construct any style of stand.

Exhibitor: As the saying goes, "half a loaf is better than no bread." I will contact the official show contractor and ask if it is possible to build our booth according to our requirements.

Information desk: Here is the contact number of the official show contractor.

Exhibitor: Thank you!

Information desk: You're welcome!

Emblem of the exposition

Qingqing, official mascot of the exposition

Unit 4 Participation in an Exhibition 参展

1. Read the conversation again and decide whether the following statements are true (T) or false (F).

(1) The organizer of the China West Tour Industry Exposition is a corporate organization, not a governmental one.   (   )

(2) The exposition is being held for the second time.   (   )

(3) The exposition will decide on only one official contractor.   (   )

(4) The official contractor will be chosen in a public bidding.   (   )

(5) There are two basic requirements for the official contractor.   (   )

(6) The official contractor will be responsible for two tasks, that is, the construction of stands and preparation for the reception of visitors.   (   )

(7) The exhibitors of this exposition will be allowed to hire their own contractor.   (   )

(8) The exhibitor from Xi'an is satisfied with the arrangement of this exposition.   (   )

2. Discuss in groups.

If you are the manager of an Exhibition Service Company, how would you prepare for the public bidding?

An exhibitor from Xi'an requires that the main tourist attractions of Xi'an should be shown to the visitors to the exposition. If your company is chosen as the official show contractor of the China West Tour Industry Exposition, how are you going to design the stand for the exhibitor coming from Xi'an? Try to form a group of four and draw a draft of the stand.

Tips: Floor space, decorations, animations, flowers, fountains, etc.

3. Match the jargons on the left with the Chinese equivalents on the right.

(1) tour industry exposition   a. 建筑面积
(2) official show contractor   b. 展台设计师
(3) show manager   c. 公开招标
(4) floor space   d. 展台
(5) public bidding   e. 展台搭建
(6) stand construction   f. 旅游产业博览会
(7) booth   g. 展览管理经理
(8) official mascot   h. 大会指定承建商
(9) exhibit designer   i. 多层展台
(10) multiple-storey exhibit   j. 吉祥物

Section Ⅱ Communication Activities

1. Pair Work

The following is included in the brochure distributed by the Information Desk of CAC Fair. Read it and with your partner ask each other questions based on the information provided in the passage.

[Sample dialogue]

A: How do we get to the Continental Exhibition Center?

B: The Continental Exhibition Center is a magnificent trade fair venue in Pazhou. We can get there by taking …

Traffic Means	Routes
by metro (subway)	Take Metro Line 2 toward Pazhou and get off at Pazhou Station (next to Xingangdong), Exit D. (The fastest way when coming from Liuhua area).
by hotel shuttle bus	All hotel buses will drive to Canton Fair Pazhou Complex via the Continental Centre. So simply ask the driver to stop. (Esp. recommended to buyers who stay in CAC Fair VFM hotels and partner hotels.)
by CAC Fair shuttle bus	Take CAC Fair free shuttle bus when coming from Canton Fair Pazhou complex or the Eastern Railway Station.
by taxi	Simply ask a taxi driver to take you to the Continental Exhibition Center by showing CAC Fair address in Chinese as below.

2. Role Play

Make up a conversation depending on the situation given below. Then act it out before the class.

[Situation]

An exhibitor from Xi'an is meeting with the official show designer of an exposition. They are talking about the stand construction. The exhibitor put forward a lot of requirements. They are working together for a final plan.

[Sample dialogue]

A: We'll display digital clocks in various shapes and colors. What's your suggestion on building the booth?

B: Since your exhibits are colorful, the background should be simple and should match all colors. White and light blue are the best choices.

A: Then what essential materials are needed?

B: Some exhibits are to be put on the walls, while some are to be placed on draping tables and glass counters. As a result, we need wooden boards, tables and glass counters.

A: How should we arrange the table and counters?

B: There should be enough space for visitors to move around. Besides looking at the exhibits, they may want to get close to the objects and feel the quality.

A: Thanks, we will construct the booth according to your advice.

[Situations]

exhibits types and colors	colorful clothing; solemn office facilities
arrangement of exhibits	hanging on the wall, garment rack(衣架), hangers(衣架)on a clothes line, stands in a row; in a set (e.g. desk, chair, pencil case can be put together)
space left out for visitors	touch the objects; look at them from a distance; take the exhibits off the wall

Section Ⅲ Expansion Reading

[导读]

每次展会都有需要遵循的展台搭建的规章制度。本文以在东莞举行的中国国际鞋展为例，阐述在展台搭建时，如何协调组展方指定承建商，以及参展商指定承建商的关系等问题。

Stand Construction—Rules and Regulations

CHINA SHOES   Deadline

CHINA SHOETEC   March, 8, 2007

Shell Scheme Package Stand

The organizer has appointed Pico IES Group Ltd. as the Official Contractor for all Shell Scheme Package booths. However, an exhibitor may employ a contractor of his choice to construct booth interiors and any freestanding displays or fittings that may be required. These must be subject to the following rules.

(1) No additional fittings or displays, including additional name board, cover, logo, balloons, etc., may be attached to the Shell Scheme booth structure. The Official Contractor reserves the right to charge the Exhibitor and his Contractor for any damage caused. If assistance is required in hanging or displaying your exhibits, please consult the Official Contractor.

(2) No painting or wallpapering of the wall panel is allowed. Exhibitors who wish to have the panels painted must inform the Official Contractor who will provide a quotation to carry out the works.

(3) Any structure that is over 2.44 meter high must be approved by the organizer. This includes towers, logos, etc..

(4) The fascia is 370 millimeter high. Exhibitors may add a company logo no higher than 250 millimeter, or more than 10 millimeter thick, by arranging with PICO.

(5) No fixing or attachment is to be made to the floor, column, wall or any other part of the building structure of the Exhibition Hall.

(6) Any change to the type or color of the floor covering provided must be applied to PICO and the cost shall be borne by the Exhibitor.

(7) No part of any structure or exhibit may extend beyond the boundaries of the space.

(8) Flashing lights/signs will not be permitted, unless they form an integral part of the Exhibitor's products.

Identification

The organizer will supply 4 contractor badges to all exhibitors' contractors for every 9 square meter of stand construction, up to a maximum of 50 badges per contractor if he/she submits the performance bond and hall management fee. All workers employed for the construction of the stand must wear contractor badges at all times when they are in the exhibition hall. Personnel without proper badge will be refused entry into the exhibition hall.

Removal of Rubbish

During the build-up period, exhibitors and their contractors will be responsible for the daily removal of construction and packaging debris off site. The exhibitor will be liable for the service fees involved in removing the debris if this is not complied.

Floor Covering

In accordance with the organizer's build-up schedule.

(1) A suitable floor covering must be provided for the stand.

(2) Carpet and main structures must be installed within 24 hours.

(3) All carpets and floor covering must be affixed with double-sided tapes. These tapes are to be removed during the dismantling period. The use of paint or adhesives on the floor of the exhibition hall is strictly forbidden.

(4) Failure to comply with these regulations may result in the delay of installation of electric and equipment move-in. Any consequential cost incurred will be charged to the exhibitor.

Open Frontages

All stands in the exhibition, irrespective of height, must have at least half of any frontage facing an aisle open.

Building Regulations

According to the local building regulations, 3 sets of construction drawings of the stand must be submitted to the organizer before the deadline, for approval by the relevant government authorities and the organizer.

1. Answer the following questions orally according to the passage.

(1) Who is the official show contractor of the exhibition of China Shoes and China ShoeTec?

(2) What is the official show contractor responsible for?

(3) What can the exhibitor's contractor do and not do?

(4) Under what situation can exhibitors put up flashing lights in the exhibition hall?

(5) What is needed for personnel to enter the exhibition hall during the process of stand construction?

(6) Who is going to bear the cost of changing the color or type of the floor covering?

(7) What does "open frontages" mean in the text?

(8) Who has the authority to approve the building plan of the booth?

2. Translate the following sentences using as many language skills learned in this lesson as possible.

(1) 在展台搭建过程中，参展商及其承建商应负责每日施工垃圾的清理工作。

(2) 垃圾应及时清理出场，否则该区域的垃圾清理费将由参展商承担。

(3) 展台结构、装饰、展品、展具或家具设备的摆设不得越过展位边界线。

(4) 所有展位，不论高度如何，其面向通道的正面部分至少有一半应向外开放。

(5) 参展商及其指定的承建商应在规定期限内向主办单位提交三套展台施工图纸。

Section Ⅳ The Internet Research

1. Search for more information about the China West Tour Industry Exposition. Try to collect more materials about 4 participating exhibitors.

2. Learn more on the Internet about 3 popular ways of constructing stands.

3. Get some information about the exhibition service companies of your city.

Section Ⅴ New Words You've Met in This Lesson

subject (to)	v.	须服从某物；受某物支配
logo	n.	商标，徽识
panel	n.	方格板，镶板
quotation	n.	报价
fascia	n.	招牌，商店入口处的名牌
attachment	n.	附件，附属物
identification	n.	许可证
submit	v.	提交，呈递
debris	n.	残骸
affix	v.	附加
tape	n.	胶带
integral	adj.	必需的，不可缺少的
installation	n.	安装
comply (with)	vi.	服从，顺从
consequential	adj.	作为结果的，相应发生的

Lesson 2

Promotion of Exhibits, Services Provided and Delegations
展品推介、会展服务及组团参展

Section Ⅰ A Sample Dialogue

[Scene] "The 2009 China Tea Industry Exposition" was going to be held. Major tea corporations from both home and abroad would participate in this show. Mr. Meng was a manager of the Longjing Tea Company, which was a new member of the exposition. He was going to the New World Exhibition Services, which was the officially designated exhibition company of this exposition. He hoped to get some useful information about products' promotion, as well as services that exhibitors could enjoy.

"2009年中国茶业博览会"将于近期举行。海内外各大茶业公司均将参展。龙井茶业公司首次参展。为了更好地推介展品并享受会展期间的服务，该公司经理孟先生前往大会指定会展服务公司——新世界会展服务公司就展品推介及会展服务事宜进行咨询。

Mr. Meng: Hello, I am Meng Hui from the Longjing Tea Company. I'm here to meet Miss Wang for some advice.

Miss Wang: Hello, Mr. Meng. I'm Wang Yan.

Mr. Meng: Nice to meet you. As it is the first time for our company to participate in the tea expo, we are eager to know how we can promote our exhibits in the show. You are an expert. I'm sure you can help me with that.

Miss Wang: As for promotion of exhibits, I would like to call your attention to one issue: staffing. Staffing plays a decisive role in promoting your products.

Mr. Meng: Can we hire some temporary staff? Our company is a little bit short-handed.

Miss Wang: It's highly recommended that you avoid using temporary staff. They usually have a limited knowledge of your products. If you really want to wrap up business deals, you have to assign expert staff, because trade visitors expect to get answers from experts.

Mr. Meng: I'll take staffing into serious consideration.

Miss Wang: What's more, you have to arrange your staff in four-hour cycles to avoid them getting tired. In order to encourage your staff, you can set some goals and give rewards to those who achieve the goals.

Mr. Meng: That's a very useful suggestion. I'll take it down in my notebook.

Miss Wang: And also, train your staff to be friendly.

Mr. Meng: Yes, that's important. By the way, I would like to know what kind of services exhibitors will enjoy during the period of the show.

Miss Wang: Our company will try the best to provide the best services to all exhibitors. For example, if exhibitors want to use conference rooms in the nearby 5-star hotel for business talks with potential buyers, we offer help to reserve rooms with the most favorable discount. Moreover, we have our labor desk there. If exhibitors require labors such as translators, interpreters, photographers, secretaries, etc., we are willing to help.

Mr. Meng: You are really considerate. I think our company will benefit from it.

Miss Wang: As for companies coming from other cities, we'll send limousines or hotel shuttle buses to pick them up at the airport.

Mr. Meng: We are worried about theft that might happen at the exhibition. I wonder if the

Unit 4 Participation in an Exhibition 参展

　　　　　　　　　security guards can protect our property.

Miss Wang: Don't worry about that. Actually theft rarely happens at the exhibition hall. The organizer will assign good security guards to protect your property. I suggest that you check your insurance policies for its coverage.

Mr. Meng: I will. Thank you for your advice and patience.

Miss Wang: It's my pleasure. By the way, you can also go to our Information Desk to ask for the floor plan. It's a map showing layout of exhibit spaces, lounges, concession areas, restrooms, electrical/plumbing accessibility, etc..

Mr. Meng: Thank you. I'll go and fetch a copy. See you.

Miss Wang: See you.

1. Read the conversation again and decide whether the following statements are true (T) or false (F).

(1) The Longjing Tea Company often attends exhibitions. (　)

(2) Staffing plays an important role in the promotion of exhibits. (　)

(3) It is recommended that exhibitors hire temporary staff to help with the show. (　)

(4) Exhibitors are advised to give rewards to staff who can achieve the goal set by the company. (　)

(5) Exhibitors have to book conference rooms themselves for business talks. (　)

(6) Exhibitors are likely to suffer from property losses because of theft. (　)

(7) It is highly advisable for exhibitors to take out an insurance policy on their exhibits. (　)

(8) Only exhibitors not coming from the local area can enjoy the service of labor desk provided by the organizer. (　)

2. Discuss in groups.

As is known to all exhibitors, staffing is very important. How do you train your staff to be prepared for the trade show? Discuss with your partner and share with each other your points of view.

There are many tea companies in Hangzhou. They are all willing to take part in the Tea Exposition. The local government decides to send a delegation to attend the exposition. What do you think are the advantages of sending delegations to participate in the trade fair? Are there any disadvantages?

3. Match the jargons on the left with the Chinese equivalents on the right.

(1) floor plan　　　　　　　　a. 组团参展

(2) staffing　　　　　　　　　b. 谈成生意

(3) labor desk　　　　　　　　c. 最优惠的折扣

(4) promote exhibits　　　　　d. 安保人员

(5) send delegations　　　　　e. 展馆平面图

(6) wrap up business deals　　f. 推介展品

(7) the most favorable discount   g. 摊位

(8) insurance coverage   h. 展台职员配置

(9) security guard   i. 展会上的劳务供应处

(10) concession area   j. 保险范围

Section Ⅱ Communication Activities

1. Pair Work

Make up a conversation depending on the situation given below. Then act it out before the class.

[Situation]

In the Tea Exposition, a trade visitor is attracted to a stand. The staff of the stand welcomes the visitor and introduces their products of specialty. In the end, the trade visitor decides to bring back some samples to his company.

[Useful expression]

(1) Hi there. I'm so happy to see you again. You are Miss Black. I remember you came to our booth on the first day of the exhibition.

(2) I'm here again because your exhibits are very appealing to me.

(3) I will send you a catalogue of our various products.

(4) I'm glad you have a good impression of our products. I'll tell my general manager about your suggestion. I hope we can keep in touch and continue to cooperate.

(5) May I know what you are interested in?

(6) How can I contact you?

(7) Our phone numbers and E-mail address are on the booklet I gave you. Please keep us informed about your selling of our products.

2. Role Play

During expos and shows, exhibitors often employ various methods to promote the exhibits. They make great efforts to attract visitors to their booths. Take turns to ask and answer according to the information below.

[Sample dialogue]

A: What methods do you know that are often used to attract visitors to the stands at shows?

B: I have seen the exhibitors use microphones, leaflets, gifts, etc. to promote the exhibits.

A: Which method do you like most? And why?

B: Patrolling team is my favorite. Once I saw a land development company trying to sell their flats by employing foreign girls. These girls wore exotic (异域的) dresses and were dancing and singing in their own language because the residential area they were trying to introduce was named Venice Villa. It is so attractive that I can even see the girls in my mind clearly today.

A: The patrolling team must have cost the exhibitor company a lot.

B: Absolutely yes. But it is worthwhile.

Methods	microphones/recorders	patrolling (巡逻) team in strange costume	brochure/leaflets	gifts
Advantages	audible (可听见的) in the large crowd	eye-catching	easy to take home	huge attraction
Disadvantages	make noise	high cost	On the spot, visitors don't have time to read it, because they are busy browsing.	high cost

Section III Expansion Reading

[导读]

此文介绍了会展期间招徕潜在客户的种种方式,其中着重分析宣传资料分发及赠品发放的正确方式。

Handouts and Giveaways that Get You Business

A key element to exhibiting sales success is your literature strategy: How do you use brochures and fliers at your show? What is it that you hand to show visitors? How do you make it effective? How do you make sure that you are not wasting your money?

At most shows you see two different literature strategy camps—the "load 'em up" people, and the "give 'em nothing" people.

Literature Can Kill Sales

If you sell a complex product, just handing out literature can prevent the purchasing process. If a prospect reviews the literature and doesn't find what they are looking for, they may think that you don't offer what they want, and then you're disqualified. In this case, it is more important to have a product expert talk to your prospect and find out what their needs are on the spot than to have them misinterpret your literature later.

Take No Literature

You may choose not to take literature to trade shows. If you have limited funds and staff, you may prefer to have the literature—only collectors keep walking. Having no literature keeps your exhibit clean and professional looking.

Bring Some Literature

If your product is easy to understand, bring the best and most appropriate literature for the show, and display sample copies. Train your sales people to review the details of your products from the literature, and use the customer's interest in your literature to secure leads you can close.

Create a Show-specific Brochure

Considering the cost of attending most shows, you may find that creating a show-specific piece for that particular audience is a good investment. You can create a piece that is concise and targeted. You can give them a copy on the spot or send them what they need after the show closes.

Be Careful in Distributing Giveaways

If your giveaway doesn't bring you customers, don't use it. If you choose to use a giveaway, make sure that you are trading the prize for your visitor's name, address, phone number and buying criteria. Get the information your sales staff needs to improve the sale. Select items that reflect the quality of your company. You don't want your logo on a cheap pen that doesn't write. One of the senseless giveaways is bottles of water. It doesn't even leave the show floor and the trashcans are littered with the sponsoring company's logo. It won't help the prospects to remember who you are when they throw away something you've given them. Select giveaways that get business. These kinds of giveaways should be something really useful, and they should be kept in a place where the prospect will refer to them when the need for your product arises. Tools make excellent giveaways. For example, a plastic slide ruler is most welcome for every stand visitor.

Make visitors earn the giveaways. Qualify visitors with a controlled giveaway. People will stand in line for T-shirts, hats, and sunglasses. Ask the visitor to complete a questionnaire, or have the visitor listen to a presentation to qualify for the prize.

1. Answer the following questions orally according to the passage.

(1) According to the passage, what is helpful to get your business on the spot of an exhibition?

(2) What are the two types of literature strategy camps?

(3) Explain the implied meanings of "load'em up" and "give'em nothing"?

(4) Under what circumstances should the exhibitor bring no literature?

(5) Under what circumstances should the exhibitor bring some literature?

(6) What is a show-specific brochure of your company?

(7) According to the passage, how can you select a suitable giveaway for potential buyers?

(8) How will you manage your giveaways to get your business?

2. Translate the following sentences using as many language skills learned in this lesson as possible.

(1) 要想在展会上吸引潜在客户，就必须利用正确的资料发放策略。

(2) 如果参展商提供的产品资料不符合潜在客户的要求，那它将失去客户。

(3) 在展会上使用最合适的产品资料宣传产品并展示产品样本。

(4) 发放赠品可能会吸引来大批顾客。

(5) 有些参展商发放赠品是为了获得顾客的个人资料，以及了解他们的喜好。

Section Ⅳ The Internet Research

1. Search for more information about the China Tea Industry Exposition. Try to collect data of 3 participating exhibitors.

2. Learn more on the Internet and draw the floor plan of an exhibition.

3. Go online to find at least 3 skills about products promotion. *http://www.wtojob.com* is a good website to browse through.

Section V New Words You've Met in This Lesson

temporary	adj.	临时的
short-handed	adj.	人手不够的
limousine	n.	豪华大巴
plumbing accessibility	n.	管路系统使用
brochure	n.	宣传册
literature	n.	文字资料
strategy	n.	策略，手腕
handout	n.	小册子
misinterpret	v.	误释
prospect	n.	前景，预期
questionnaire	n.	问卷；调查
concise	adj.	准确的，精确的
litter	v.	乱扔垃圾

Section VI Writing Related to EC Industry

1. What promotional literature like?

For most of the time, exhibitors have to take copies of the promotional literature of their bestsellers(畅销品) along with them to exhibitions. Such literature is supposed to include the serial number and name of the product, images, characteristics and technique parameters of the product. It aims at showing visitors a whole picture of the product.

2. Sample writing.

Sony Cyber-shot T900 Digital Camera

Characteristics:

- Easy Maintenance(维护，保养);
- Modernized Design;
- Excellent Reliability & High Stability;
- One-year Limited Warranty(保修).

Technique Parameters

max resolution	4 000×3 000 (12 megapixel)
sensor size (type)	1/2.3" (CCD)
zoom capability	4×optical＋2×digital

focal length	35～140 mm
max. aperture	F3.5～F4.6
supports conversion lenses	No
auto focus	Yes
optical image stabilization	Yes
built-in flash	Yes
manual control	Exposure compensation
movie mode	Yes
sound recording	Yes
storage method	11 MB onboard memory＋memory stick duo

3. Discuss with your partner and design a copy of promotional literature (e.g. a pamphlet, or a brochure) of a product that you know well.

Lesson 3

Emergencies during the Exhibition
会展期间突发情况

Section Ⅰ A Sample Dialogue

[Scene] As the 2009 Flower Exposition was going to open in a few days, Mr. Li, the show manager of the New World Exhibition Services, was very busy helping his customers—from exhibit managers to participating florists—with the problems they might face. He looked around the exhibition hall to check whether the exhibits had already arrived after the construction of stands.

2009 年花卉博览会开幕在即，新世界展览服务公司的展览管理经理李先生忙着帮助来自各个参展花卉商的展出经理们解决他们面对的各种问题，认真检查参展商的展品在展台搭建之后是否已经到场。

Mr. Li: Hi, I am Li Li, the show manager of this exhibition. Is everything going well in your stand?

Exhibit Manager: Yes. I am getting worried about our exhibits.

Mr. Li: Oh, what happened? Is there anything that I can do to help?

Exhibit Manager: You know, our stand has already been set up. Next we are to move in our exhibits. In fact most of our exhibits have arrived except for one very

	important orchid plant, which can be considered as the "gem" of our company. We planned to use it to attract the attention of trade visitors.
Mr. Li:	You mean the plant hasn't arrived yet? Maybe you can wait a little longer for it.
Exhibit Manager:	It was supposed to arrive with the other exhibits. I am worried that it might have been lost on the way.
Mr. Li:	That would be terrible! By the way, did you use honest freight forwarders?
Exhibit Manager:	Of course we did. Since the orchid was priceless, we hired the EEC freight forwarder, one of the best in our country. Now other plants and potted flowers are here. Where's the orchid?
Mr. Li:	Don't worry. To find it, we have a few steps to follow. First, contact the EEC freight forwarder immediately to learn how they delivered all your exhibits. Second, remember every box of delivery should have been registered with a serial number. Ask the EEC freight forwarder for the serial number of your orchid. And then you can work with the EEC to trace the orchid, using the serial number.
Exhibit Manager:	Oh, yes. Look at me, the more worried I get, the more muddle-headed I become. I'll call the EEC immediately.

(The exhibit manager is talking with the EEC clerk on the phone.)

Mr. Li:	What did they say?
Exhibit Manager:	They said they'll check the document immediately. They also asked for my stand number and company name again to see if there was any mistake in the delivery process.
Mr. Li:	I'm sure you'll get your orchid back. While tracing the orchid, remember to move in your other exhibits. Decorate your stand. Get everything prepared before the exhibition.
Exhibit Manager:	Thank you, I will.

(The next day, the exhibit manager comes to tell Mr. Li that they've found the orchid.)

Exhibit Manager:	Mr. Li, I am so happy. We've located our lost orchid.
Mr. Li:	Really, congratulations! How did you find it?
Exhibit Manager:	The EEC checked their document. One of their clerks mistyped our stand number. We went to that stand last night to get our orchid. The EEC apologized and offered to compensate us for the inconvenience they caused.
Mr. Li:	Good. Finally you get your treasure back. Now you can get down to work.

(The Exhibit Manager is talking with the manager of the EEC Company about the compensation.)

Exhibit Manager: I'm really mad about the carelessness in your work.

EEC Manager: I sincerely apologize to you for our negligence on behalf of my company. In order to relieve your stress and anxiety, my company entrusted me to talk with you about the compensation.

Exhibit Manager: I would like to listen to your suggestion concerning the compensation.

EEC Manager: As is covered in the insurance policy, your losses will be refunded by the insurance company. As your losses are mild, the compensation will not be too much.

Exhibit Manager: That sounds reasonable. How can I get the compensation?

EEC Manager: You will get the money within 30 days. We will compensate you by wire transfer. We hope it will minimize your losses.

Exhibit Manager: How considerate! I will take your compensation plan.

EEC Manager: That's the deal. Let's keep in touch.

Exhibit Manager: All right. I'll go to the site tomorrow. Thank you!

1. Read the conversation again and decide whether the following statements are true (T) or false (F).

(1) The exhibitor in the dialogue lost all his exhibits.　　　　　　　　　(　)

(2) The loss of his exhibit was caused by his failure to use a responsible freight forwarder.　　　　　　　　　　　　　　　　　　　　　　　　　　　(　)

(3) With the help of the serial number, the lost exhibit can be traced.　　(　)

(4) The exhibitor gave the EEC freight forwarder the wrong stand number, so the forwarder failed to deliver the exhibit to the right place.　　　　　　　　　(　)

(5) The exhibitor can't get any compensation because it is his fault.　　(　)

(6) The exhibitor has to cancel his stand because his orchid can't be found.　(　)

(7) The organizer has to compensate for the losses caused by the missing orchid.　(　)

(8) The exhibitor will get a compensation of a large sum.　　　　　　(　)

2．Discuss in groups.

A successful conference partly results from good emergency management. The show manager has to face a lot of unexpected problems throughout the period of the show. In order to deal with all kinds of situations well, what should be done prior to the exhibition by the organizer to get prepared for any emergent situation?

Several years ago, the SARS broke out in Beijing, the capital of China. When the epidemic just began to spread, many conferences were still going on. If you were a show manager at one international conference, how would you handle the emergency situation? How would you organize all of the exhibitors?

3. Match the jargons on the left with the Chinese equivalents on the right.

(1) florist　　　　　　　　　　　　　　　　　a. 送货

(2) freight forwarder   b. 展会取消
(3) the serial number   c. 发现踪迹
(4) delivery   d. 注册费
(5) get a trace of   e. 花商
(6) exhibition cancellation   f. 货运代理企业
(7) refund   g. 电汇
(8) registration fee   h. 编号
(9) space rental fee   i. 退款
(10) wire transfer   j. 展位租赁费

Section Ⅱ Communication Activities

1. Pair Work

Make up a conversation depending on the situation given below. Then act it out before the class.

[Situation] In the Flower Exposition, an exhibitor's valuable potted landscape(盆景) was stolen last night. The exhibitor complains to the show manager about his losses and insecurities. The show manager tries to solve this problem.

A:　Exhibitor

B:　Show Manager

[Useful Expression]

(1) We should report to the local police in the first place. Let them conduct an investigation.

(2) You must have insured your priceless potted plant. Contact your insurance company to see if you can get compensation.

(3) The organizer will be liable for your losses.

2．Role Play

Student A: The organizer

Student B: The exhibitor

[Sample dialogue]

A:　Hello, is that Mr. Sun with ABC Machinery Tools Company. This is Wang calling on behalf of the South-west Exhibiting Company. I regret to inform you of the cancellation of our exhibition.

B:　You must be kidding. What's happening? We have done a lot to get ready for it.

A:　Because of the large-scale labor strike(大规模罢工) in this area, we have to cancel the show to ensure the safety.

B:　That's unexpected. My company has spent a lot on it. You know, the cancellation will result in a big loss in our company.

A:　We understand. Don't worry about your losses. We will talk about the loss issue via e-mail and telephone calls later. Please take care.

B: OK, you too.

[Situations]

A	B
It's raining cats and dogs in our area for a week. Some of the exhibition facilities are soaked and cannot function properly.	Air-flights were booked, and deposits were paid in advance for hotel reservation.
Unidentified terrorists have made threats of explosions and attack. Put the show off to another time.	Rearrange the flights.
Earthquakes cause communication failure. There may be minor quakes.	Arrived exhibits are damaged; and preparation expenses would be wasted.
There is wide-spread disease. Government does not encourage population mobility/ human flow.	We have done a lot of preparatory work, for example, our exhibits have been shipped to the destination.

Section Ⅲ Expansion Reading

[导读]

提前制订会展期间突发情况的危机处理方案，以不变应万变。一份危机处理计划包括可能发生的危机的类型、处理方式及赔偿问题等。

Disaster Plans

No one wants or expects a disaster, but planning for the worst will ensure your show weathers the storm.

A Good Plan Addresses Every Possibility

(1) Natural disasters (hurricanes, tornadoes, floods, earthquakes, snow or ice storms).

(2) Facility issues (power failure, fires, structural issues).

(3) Health issues (flu or SARS; food poisoning).

(4) Potential dangers (chemical spills or mold).

(5) Labor strikes (transportation, convention facility or hotels).

(6) Political demonstrations (protestors in a general session or on the show floor).

(7) Terrorist acts or threats of terrorism, bomb threats.

(8) Transportation issues (airline strikes, trucking strikes, airports closed, trains or subways down).

(9) Closures ordered by government or travel restrictions, declaration of war.

What to Put in the Plan

(1) List names and cell numbers of all key staff, site personnel and contractor, as well as your insurance agent's contact information. (Radios are essential if cell service goes down.)

(2) Spell out step-by-step what's to be done and who should be contacted by which staff in various situations.

(3) List the designated emergency meeting areas for staff both inside and outside the building and in the chief hotel.

(4) Include specific wording for messages to audiences if a disruption/ emergency occurs on site.

(5) Provide a form to report incidents. Designate where such forms will be available on site.

(6) Provide floor diagrams marked with exits and house phones for calling into facility offices.

Training

(1) Relevant staff and vendors should meet to review the emergency plan together before the event to ensure all are aware of their responsibilities.

(2) On site, require staff to familiarize them with exits, stairwells, elevators, and optional back-of-house exits if required.

(3) Practice getting to designated meeting areas. During set-up, radio all key personnel to gather immediately and time the drill.

(4) Hold a training session for volunteers in charge of particular areas to be sure they know appropriate exits, procedures and wording for instructions.

Who Gets a Copy of the Plan

(1) Show director/manager.

(2) Exhibit sales team.

(3) Key on-site staff or vendors (registration, IT and AV).

(4) Contractor liaison.

(5) Building liaison.

(6) Organization CEO.

(7) On-site volunteers/moderators who may be in charge of areas involving large groups (such as a general session).

(8) PR staff.

(9) Call center for exhibitors and/or attendees.

Basic Lessons

(1) Go over your disaster plan before each show. Create a model plan and update it with specific names and phone numbers relevant to each show.

(2) Be as calm as possible in all actions and communications.

(3) Take care of people and property first. Worry about assessing blame and responsibility later.

(4) Submit your plan to your hotels and get recommendations (such as evacuation routes and how to obey their procedures).

(5) Know what's in each of your vendor contracts about notices of cancellations, refunds, deposits and penalties related to cancellation; and provisions for rescheduling.

(6) Communicate with all stakeholders regularly via web sites, e-mails or phone. Be honest. If you're working on a revised location or date, say so but wait to announce the facts when they're clear.

(7) After you've endured a disaster or event cancellation, hold a roundtable discussion or conference with key players to review lessons learned.

Who Decides Whether the Show Can Go On?

(1) In cases of natural disasters or facility problems, the owner of the convention center (often a municipality or other government entity) determines that the venue is unsafe or unusable, and communicates to show management that the show cannot be hosted.

(2) Show organizers may decide in cases such as health issues or airline strikes that may prevent attendance. Depending on the organization, the show director, CEO or an association board of directors may make the decision.

(3) Note, often it's a case of, "he who cancels bears the liability," so conference centers may be hesitant to say they can't host an event. Depending on the timing it may be wise for a show organizer to prepare back-up options while waiting for the conference center to make the call in the event of a labor strike.

1. Answer the following questions orally according to the passage.

(1) What possibilities should be pre-considered in a plan?

(2) What should be included in a good plan for disruptions?

(3) Who is going to get a copy of the disaster plan prior to the exhibition?

(4) How do you prepare convention staff and volunteer for an emergent situation?

(5) What should the convention staff do if there is a terrorist attack happening near the convention hall?

(6) What should be taken care of when emergency takes place?

(7) Who can decide whether the convention stopped by emergency should be continued or not?

(8) If a convention is cancelled, who is to pay for the losses?

2. Translate the following sentences using as many language skills learned in this lesson as possible.

(1) 如果会议期间出现通信故障问题，请及时联系大会主办方。

(2) 一份完备的突发情况处理计划必须涵盖一切可能发生的危机，如自然灾害、传染病暴发、大罢工等。

(3) 在危机处理计划中必须写明大会工作人员及承建商的姓名、手机号码，以及大会指定保险公司的联系信息。

(4) 大会主办方处理完突发情况之后应及时召开圆桌会议，总结经验教训，探讨更好的解决方式。

(5) 根据会展经验之谈，任何会展，不论规模大小，都必须投保以策万全。

Section Ⅳ The Internet Research

1. Search for information about at least 2 examples of detailed disaster management scheme on-line.

2. Find on-line what types of emergencies organizers may encounter in the exhibition.

3. Compare the western way of emergency management with the Chinese way. Try to learn from the comparison.

Section V New Words You've Met in This Lesson

orchid	n.	兰花
gem	n.	宝物
negligence	n.	疏忽
disrupt	v.	扰乱，打断
mold	n.	霉菌
designate	v.	指定，任命
demonstration	n.	游行，示威
protestor	n.	抗议者
terrorism	n.	恐怖主义
vendor	n.	卖主，摊贩
liaison	n.	联络，联系；联络人
moderator	n.	调解人，监督人
on-site	adj.	现场的，在场的
stakeholder	n.	利益相关者
liability	n.	(法律上的)责任

Section VI Review of This Unit

1. Jargons in This Unit

tour industry exposition	旅游产业博览会
official show contractor	大会指定承建商
public bidding	公开招标
official mascot	大会吉祥物
multiple-storey exhibit	多层展台
shell scheme package stand	标准展位
performance bond	施工押金
booth interior	展台内部
open frontage	开放的正面；面对公众的展台正面
labor desk	展会劳务供应处
the most favorable discount	最优惠的折扣
insurance coverage	保险范围
giveaway	赠品

续表

refund	退款
wire transfer	电汇
deposit	定金
penalty	处罚、罚款

2. Sentence Patterns/Practical Dialogues

(1) I would like to know what the basic requirements are for the official show contractor.

(2) Well, there are some requirements. First, … Second, …Last, …

(3) How should we arrange …?

(4) There should be enough space for visitors to…

(5) Thanks, we'll construct the booth according to your advice.

(6) I'm glad you have a good impression of …Please keep us informed about …

(7) May I know what you are interested in?

(8) How can I contact you?

(9) What methods do you know that are often used to…?

(10) Is everything going on well in your stand?

(11) Yes, it is going quite well. / No, I'm afraid not.

(12) I regret to inform you of…

(13) How can I get the compensation?

(14) The losses from cancellation will be refunded by the insurance company. You will get the compensation within 30 days.

3. Writing Related to EC Industry

Design a copy of promotional literature.

Unit 5

Cancellation and Move-out
退展和撤展

单元目标

1. 了解退展程序,维护自己的利益,追讨定金。
2. 把握撤展过程及后续工作。
3. 了解撤展后评估方法。
4. 正确阅读并理解撤展通知,掌握其写法。

Lesson 1

Cancellation of Exhibit Registration
取消预订展位

Section I A Sample Dialogue

[Scene] Two exhibitors called the sales department of Beijing Rayon Exhibition Company to ask about terms of cancellation of exhibition registration. Mark explained the details to them.

两位参展商打电话到北京瑞阳展览公司销售部，咨询有关取消预定展位的信息，马克做了详细的解答。

Exhibitor 1: Could you tell me what I will do if I'm not able to attend the exhibition?

Mark: You may cancel the registration and inform us either by letter, fax, telephone call, or e-mail.

Exhibitor 1: How much notice is required for cancellation?

Mark: It depends. Whenever you send a notice of cancellation, you will be liable for all or part of the cost incurred on your behalf if you have signed the contract.

Exhibitor 1: Can you tell me more about it?

Mark: Yes. If we receive your written notice between 120 and 61 days before the show, we will send you a 50% refund. If we receive it 60 days or less before the show, there will be no refund at all.

Exhibitor 1: How do I cancel my registration if I have not sent my money yet?

Mark: In that case, the contract is not effective, so we don't charge you for anything. But we won't keep the space number for you any longer.

Exhibitor 1: Oh, I know. Thank you very much for the information.

Mark: You're welcome. We're always at your service.

Exhibitor 1: Goodbye.

Mark: Bye. Thanks for calling.

(Later, the telephone rang again, so Mark picked up the phone.)

Mark: Good morning. Beijing Rayon Exhibition. How can I help you?

Exhibitor 2: I made a reservation for the High-tech Exhibition six months ago. I will not be able to attend it, so I'd like to cancel my registration.

Mark: May I have your name, please?

Unit 5 Cancellation and Move-out 退展和撤展

Exhibitor 2: I'm William Smith with American Packaging Machinery Manufacturers Institute China office.
Mark: Let me check. Please wait for a moment. Yes, you have reserved a booth and the booth number is GO98. Am I right?
Exhibitor 2: Yes, you're right.
Mark: We won't accept your cancellation unless you send us a written notice by the end of this month. And then you may receive a 40% refund from us.
Exhibitor 2: Well, that's better than nothing. When can you mail the refund to me?
Mark: According to the company's regulation, I will mail the cancellation refund to you when the show is over. I hope you understand.
Exhibitor 2: That's understandable. Thank you.
Mark: You're welcome. We look forward to your participation in our next show.
Exhibitor 2: Goodbye.
Mark: Goodbye.

1. Read the conversation again and decide whether the following statements are true (T) or false (F).

(1) The first exhibitor called to cancel his registration and ask for a refund. (   )
(2) The second exhibitor made a reservation for the High-tech Exhibition two months ago. (   )
(3) A full amount of registration fee will be returned to both of the two exhibitors. (   )
(4) The exhibitor is liable for the contract once the registration fee has been sent to the organizer. (   )
(5) If the second exhibitor sends the cancellation notice after the end of this month, he will receive a 40% refund. (   )
(6) As a rule, after the show the refund will be sent to the exhibitor who has cancelled the show registration. (   )
(7) Exhibitors can cancel a reservation through e-mail or phone. (   )
(8) The sooner the exhibitor sends out the written notice of cancellation, the more money he can receive for his refund. (   )

2. Discuss in groups and then present the idea in class.

(1) How is the registration for a booth in an exhibition canceled?
(2) What are done to avoid forfeit deposit to the least degree?
(3) What are the tips for the exhibitors who can't attend a reserved exhibition?

3. Match the jargons on the left with the Chinese equivalents on the right.

(1) call off   a. 解约条款
(2) cancellation money   b. 没收押金
(3) lost profit   c. 参展报名序号
(4) costs incurred on behalf of sb.   d. 利润损失

(5) registration number
(6) termination clause
(7) forfeit deposit
(8) nonrefundable

e. 不可退还的
f. 取消
g. 由某人引起的费用
h. 解约金

Section II Communication Activities

1. Pair Work

Make dialogues with your partner to deal with the following cases by using the background information.

[Sample dialogue]

A: Hello, this is the Organizing Committee of Beijing Hi-tech Exhibition.

B: Hello, this is Woodson Jin from the Shell Oil Company.

A: What can I do for you?

B: I reserved a booth in your exhibition. What can I do if I'm not able to attend the exhibition?

A: Well, the exhibition will open on May 12, 2009. Today it is April 9, 2009. According to our contract, cancellation 60 days or less before the show will result in a forfeit deposit.

B: Oh, I see. I will call back later and tell you my decision. Thank you very much!

A: It's my pleasure.

[Situations]

(1) David Brown calls to confirm the accurate amount, and booth number of the reservation before sending the money.

(2) David Brown calls to cancel the registration on December 10, 2008, and asks about how much money he can get back from the exhibition organizer.

(3) David Brown calls to reserve another 9-square-meter stand on January 9, 2009, and asks about how much money he has to pay as a deposit.

[Background Information]

A: Service staff   B: Mr. David Brown

Space Application Form of Beijing Hi-tech Exhibition

May 12-20, 2009   Beijing

Company: Star Toy Company	Contact Person: David Brown		
Address: 45# Flower Street, New York, USA	Zip: AB 2987		
Tel: 35697532	Fax: 35697533		
E-mail: startoy@hotmail.cn	Website: www.startoy.cn		
Package Stand 9 m²/unit	¥2,500/unit	2 unit(s)	Total ¥5,000
Package Stand 6 m²/unit	¥1,700/unit	1 unit(s)	Total ¥1,700

Unit 5 Cancellation and Move-out 退展和撤展

续表

Attendance	A: ¥1,800 per person B: ¥2,800 per person	A:2 B:1	Total ¥6,400
Incidental Expense(杂费)	¥300 per person	3person(s)	Total ¥900
Service Fee	¥3,000/unit	3unit(s)	Total ¥9,000

In the event of the organizer agreeing to any request from the contract, the exhibitor will be liable for all or part of the cost stated in the contract in accordance with the following regulations:

Cancellation 271 days or more before the show	15%
Cancellation between 270 days and 181 days before the show	40%
Cancellation between 180 days and 121 days before the show	60%
Cancellation between 120 days and 61 days before the show	80%
Cancellation 60 days or less before the show	Forfeit deposit

Total: ¥23,000

Advance deposit: ¥10,000

Signature: David Brown   Date: July 7, 2008

2. Role Play

Suppose you are unable to attend a trade fair for which you have paid the deposit several months ahead of time. A clerk from the conference center is explaining to you how you can cancel it. Some tips are given below.

Cancelling attendance	Response
I'd like to cancel my registration. There is no other choice, so I have to cancel. I won't be able to attend, so I need to cancel. Is there any possibility of calling off my registration? Is it too late for me to cancel my registration?	The show is in less than a month, but if you insist we can work it out with you. Yes, what's your booth number?
Asking about terms of cancellation	**Response**
What is your company's cancellation date policy? What do I do if I need to cancel? How do I cancel my registration? I need to cancel. How to do it?	You will be asked to pay a cancellation fee varying from the dates we receive your notice prior to the cancelling date. What is your registration number? In that case, the contract is not effective, so we don't charge you for anything.
How much do you charge for cancelling my registration? I'd like to get a refund because I can't participate in the show. I will not be going for some reason so I want to get my money back.	There will be a 50% refund. You will receive the refund after the show.

Section Ⅲ Expansion Reading

[导读]

展会合同在展会的组织和运作过程中起着至关重要的作用，它规定主展方和参展方的权利和义务。下面是2007年中国(深圳)房地产国际展览会暨深圳秋季房交会的展会合同摘要。

**2007 China (Shenzhen) Housing Industry International Exposition
& Shenzhen (autumn) Real Estate Trade Fair**

September 29 – October 3

Shenzhen Convention & Exhibition Center, Shenzhen

Exhibition Contract

This Contract is made the _____ (day) of _____ (month), _____ (year) between Party A (organizer) <u>Shenzhen Real Estate Consultation Co., Ltd.</u> and Party B (exhibitor) for the Exhibition titled <u>2007 China (Shenzhen) Housing Industry International Exposition And Shenzhen (autumn) Real estate Trade Fair</u>.

Whereas Party B confirms to attend 2007 China (Shenzhen) Housing Industry International Exposition And Shenzhen (autumn) Real Estate Trade Fair (hereinafter referred to as 2007 China Housing Expo.), rent booths and book advertisement under this Contract; the parties agree as follows:

Exhibiting Company
Company Name _____
Contact Person _____
Address   _____
City _____ Country _____ Postcode _____
Telephone _____ Fax _____
E-mail _____ Website _____

Location
Exhibition Hall 1, Shenzhen Convention & Exhibition Center
Shenzhen Conference & Exhibition Center (hereinafter referred to as SZCEC), 3rd Fuhua Road, Futian District, Shenzhen, China.

Exhibition Space
Please check all choices that apply:

Space type	Quality	Price	Total costs
☐ Standard booth(9m^2/booth)	_____	_____ RMB/booth	_____
☐ Bare land(minimal 36m^2)	_____	_____ RMB/m^2	_____

Total amount: RMB_____

Exhibition Management Deposit

Real estate: RMB_____Others: RMB_____(Per booth or every 9m^2)

Total: RMB_____

The deposit should return to Party B on the working day after the withdrawal date in the case of HIS behavior according to this Contract, the exhibition rules, the laws, and any other rules of organizing committee during the exhibition, or should not be refunded on HIS disobeying those rules to make up the loss of Party A. If such Deposit is not enough to make up for the loss, Party A shall be entitled to exercise its recourse for the payable balance against Party B.

Payment

The total of the above mentioned fee: RMB_____

Account name: Shenzhen Land And Real Estate Exchange Center

Account No.: 032002610056968

Opening bank: China Construction Bank, Shenzhen Branch, Zhenhua Sub-branch

Party B agrees to sign the contract and pay the earnest RMB_____only (RMB_____per standard or every 9m^2) at the date of confirming the booth, and should remit the balance RMB_____only (in words RMB_____) within 5 working days form the signing date to the account above mentioned.

Exhibition Set-up and Break Down

1. Party B shall be liable for the booth decoration & removal, products exhibition & sale within the booth, and shall not occupy the passages and upper space of the fair. Otherwise, Party A shall give a written notice of breach of the exhibition rules to Party B, and the exhibition management deposit paid by Party B shall not be refunded.

2. Booths in the north area shall not exceed the height limit of 5 meters. Those in the south area shall not exceed 7 meters. Those close to the wind tower under D160 and D200 exhibition groups shall not exceed the height limit of 5 meters (subject to the plan of the exhibit booths as shown by Party A). Otherwise, Party A shall give a written notice of breach of the exhibition rules to Party B, and the exhibition management deposit paid by Party B shall not be refunded.

Performance of Contract

If any dispute occurs during the performance of this contract, Party A and Party B shall settle it through negotiation. If both Parties cannot settle such a dispute through negotiation, either Party shall be entitled to take action with the people's court.

1. This Contract is made out in Chinese and English. There are four copies, two for each party. All four shall be equally authentic.

2. This Contract shall come into existence after it is signed by both Parties. It shall take effect when Party B pays off the costs of the exhibit booth, exhibition management deposit within the time limit as stated in this Contract.

Party A:	Party B:
Shenzhen Real Estate Consultation Co., Ltd	Legal representative (signature):
Legal representative (signature):	Authorized agent (signature):
Authorized agent (signature):	

1. Read the contract again and decide whether the following statements are true (T) or false (F).

(1) This exposition is organized by Shenzhen Government.　　　　　　　(　)

(2) Industrial commodities are on show in this exposition.　　　　　　　(　)

(3) Within 7 days the exhibitors shall pay the money after signing the contract.　(　)

(4) All the booths in this exhibition are as tall as 6 meters.　　　　　　　(　)

(5) The organizer will decorate all of the booths for the exhibitors.　　　　(　)

(6) If the exhibitor occupies the passages or the upper space of the fair, the organizer will not refund his exhibition management deposit.　　　　　　　　　　　　　(　)

(7) This contract is written both in English and Chinese.　　　　　　　(　)

(8) The contract has two copies, one for the organizer and the other for the exhibitor.　(　)

2. Translate the following sentences using as many language skills learned in this lesson as possible.

A：早上好，我是上海大通贸易公司的销售部经理。我要取消六个月前的参展报名。

B：哦，太可惜了。现在离展览开幕还不到一个月。

A：实在对不起，由于一些产品的技术原因，我们确实无法参加。

B：那好吧。根据合同规定，我们要从押金中扣除60%的解约费。

A：哦，你可以把剩下的钱寄回给我吗？

B：请问你的预订展台号是多少？

A：我们的预订展台是E039。

B：那好，我们会把剩余的押金寄给你的。

A：请问何时我能收到退款。

B：根据规定，要在展览结束后才能把钱寄过去。

Section Ⅳ　The Internet Research

1. Research the Internet after class to look for contracts concerning cancelling registration both in Chinese and English. List at least five phrases you learned.

2. Research the Internet after class to get at least 5 tips for reserving a booth in an exhibition.

Section Ⅴ　New Words You've Met in This Lesson

confirm	vi.	确认，证实
registration	n.	定位，注册

续表

cancellation	n.	取消
confirm	vt.	确定
expense	n.	花费，开销
party	n.	(契约，或争论中的)一方，当事人
hereinafter	adv.	以下
remit	vt.	汇寄
recourse	n.	求助的对象
liable	adj.	负责的
exceed	vt.	超过
authentic	adj.	真实的
signature	n.	签字

Lesson 2

Move-out
撤　展

Section Ⅰ　A Sample Dialogue

[Scene] After the exhibition, Miss Jiang is expressing her appreciation to Alice, who is a member of the organizing committee of the exhibition and has been a great help to Miss Jiang. At the same time, Miss Jiang is busy preparing to return to China.

在参加展览会后，江小姐准备在回国前向主办方成员艾丽丝表达诚挚的感谢。

Miss Jiang: Thank you for your help during the exhibition, Alice. Without your help, I could hardly have met so many clients in this exhibition. Thank you very much.
Alice: It's my pleasure.
Miss Jiang: I like this booth very much, and I plan to take part in the exhibition next year, too.
Alice: We will inform you of next year's exhibition in advance and reserve this booth for you.
Miss Jiang: That's very kind of you.
Alice: I appreciate your way of doing business. If there is anything else I can do to help you, please don't hesitate to let me know.

Miss Jiang: In fact, there is something I am still not sure about.

Alice: Please tell me. What is it?

Miss Jiang: What should I do with the display items?

Alice: You can sell some of the display items. For those that you cannot sell here, you can find a transportation company to ship them back to your country.

Miss Jiang: That sounds good. Which transportation company do you recommend?

Alice: The organizers of the exhibition have already appointed a few transportation companies in the exhibition manual. Look, here are their telephone numbers.

Miss Jiang: Thank you. I will call them in a moment.

1. Read the conversation again and decide whether the following statements are true (T) or false (F).

(1) Miss Jiang thanked Alice for introducing many clients to her. ( )

(2) Alice reserved the booth for Miss Jiang. ( )

(3) Miss Jiang feels satisfied with the booth. ( )

(4) Miss Jiang will attend the exhibition next year. ( )

(5) Miss Jiang has sold out all the display items. ( )

(6) Miss Jiang has to take all the display items back home by herself. ( )

(7) The organizers of the exhibition suggested several transportation companies to the exhibitors. ( )

(8) Alice has established a good relationship with Miss Jiang. ( )

2. Select the correct words and phrases to fill in the blanks. Remember to change the forms if necessary.

| move out | in advance | express appreciation | appoint | reserve |

(1) If you want to get back your down payment of a booth, you should inform the organizing committee _____.

(2) After the show, many exhibitors are busy preparing to _____.

(3) Up to now, all the booths for the Auto Show have been _____ by exhibitors at home and abroad.

(4) Don't forget to _____ to the staff who have given you a hand.

(5) The organizers _____ ten shipping companies before the exhibition was opened.

3. Match the jargons on the left with the Chinese equivalents on the right.

(1) display item   a. 撤展

(2) move-out   b. 提前

(3) transportation company   c. 运输公司

(4) exhibition manual   d. 参展手册

(5) in advance   e. 展品

(6) storage area
(7) pack
(8) express appreciation

f. 打包
g. 表达感谢
h. 存储区

Section II Communication Activities

1. Pair Work

Practice the dialogues with your partner.

A: A staff of the exhibiting company   B: An exhibitor

[Sample dialogue]

A: Sir, what can I do for you? You look so worried.

B: Oh. I reserved plants and flowers to decorate my booth online from Sunny Flowers Company, but I have been waiting for them to arrive the whole morning.

A: Did you call the company?

B: Yes, but the number doesn't work. I have only two hours left, and as you see my booth is still a mess.

A: Don't worry! We have business with the company. If you'd like I will give them a call for you.

B: That would be fantastic!

A: (*Dialing the phone.*) Hello! Is that Sunny Flowers Company? (*Giving the phone to B.*)

B: (*Speaking to the phone.*) Hello, I need two hundred roses and one hundred lilies in two hours.

B: (*Speaking to the staff.*) Thank you so much!

A: You're welcome.

[Situations]

(1) You are worried about moving exhibits into the booth.

(2) You wish to have a look at the goods in the storage area.

(3) You need somebody's help to pack the exhibits.

(4) You find your booth is not cool enough, even when the central air-conditioning system is working.

2. Role Play

(1) At the end of the show, Mr. Steven from ABC Company is talking to Mr. Zhang from a transportation company about the dismantling and transportation affairs.

Mr. Steven	Mr. Zhang
Wants to ship his goods back home	Asks about the place and tells price
Needs help with the move-out	Asks about the time and tells price
Bargains	Anti-bargains
Agrees	Agrees

(2) Imagine you were one of the exhibitors in a trade show. Do a post-show evaluation and report to your boss acted by your partner.

[Sample dialogue]

Mr. Huang has just participated in an international exhibition. He is talking about the results of the exhibition with the General Manager, Mr. Li.

L: Mr. Huang, what are the results of the exhibition?

H: Not bad.

L: Could you give me some details?

H: We have established business relationships with two new clients, who ordered ¥20 million of silk skirts.

L: Good.

H: I also got acquainted with more than 200 customers.

L: Oh, wow.

H: Customers made more than ten suggestions. There, I held a press conference to introduce our products. As a result, our brand has been strengthened.

L: Very good!

H: Here is the results analysis. I hope the visitors at the exhibition can be our real buyers in 3 to 6 months. What's more, we learned a lot from other exhibitors.

L: You are right. I think you've done an excellent job.

[Situations]

Name of exhibition	product	Orders	Customers
Shanghai Clothing Exhibition	women's clothes	3 big orders	300
Guangzhou Toy Fair	stuffed toys	5 overseas orders	200
Chongqing Machinery Exhibition	gears	2 new orders	400
Beijing Food Exhibition	tea	7 orders from new overseas markets	200

Section Ⅲ Expansion Reading

[导读]

展览会后常常被忽略的是展后评估和针对会展中获得的信息开展后续工作。如果能够养成将展览会效果与预期目标比较的习惯,将有助于较准确地预测未来展览会的效果。

Post-show Evaluation & Follow-up

Exhibitors often forget to follow up the visitors who have come to their stands in time, not to mention conducting a post-show evaluation. Most trade show exhibitors fail to do the follow-up activities for a couple of reasons.

(1) You return to the office to find your inbox full of emails, your voicemail is overflowing

and you need check your current projects and sales.

(2) You always think that all the people you've met at the trade show will call you, because you have given them a brochure and they are certain to remember you.

No doubt, you will have some catch-up to do after the trade show but the key to success is to place your post-show activities in the first place. First, follow up all urgent issues immediately. Second, deal with issues that have come up with existing clients while you were away. Do not give up existing clients for potential new clients.

Follow up Immediately

Post-show planning includes a multiple contact plan. Call the most serious prospects first. You should follow up with all of your leads within 48 hours of the show by email or phone. Continue to use good sales techniques to develop a professional relationship.

Email all booth visitors who provided contact information (regardless of whether they are good prospects or not).

(1) Say "Thank you" for stopping by your booth.

(2) Extend the offer of the trade show.

(3) Offer your products/service solutions.

With qualified prospects, still send an email, but also state that you will call to arrange a time to meet or discuss the next steps.

Categorize Trade Show Leads

If you've done the trade show properly, you should have written down certain important things, such as what the leads want, connections that you've made with them and urgent things to do. Separate these from the rest of the leads and start with them first. If you have indeed made that connection at the trade show, you will likely be remembered the next day. Most trade show exhibitors often forget that not all leads should be followed up in the same way.

What happens if a trade show brings you too many leads? That's a nice problem to have. You still want to keep in touch with all of them, to preserve as many business opportunities as possible. Consider a post-show letter or email follow-up. By using an integrated system like Microsoft Word or Constant Contact, you can turn out a pretty nice "personalized" note to each of them. You might tell the reader that you will be in contact with them within the next couple weeks.

Evaluate the Trade Show

In addition to following up with leads obtained at your trade show, one of the most important post-show activities is to conduct an analysis. By answering some basic questions you will identify things that will help you when planning future events. Some of the key questions to ask are:

(1) What worked?

(2) What didn't work?

(3) Was the booth functional?

(4) Was the booth in the right location?

(5) Was this the right trade show for my business?
(6) Did I meet the right people?
(7) What did I learn from others?
(8) What did I learn about the competition?

Six to twelve month is a proper time to measure and determine the long-term profits brought by a show. At some point, you have to determine that you cannot participate in every trade show that comes along. Therefore, it is imperative that you determine which trade shows give you the best performance.

1. Read the conversation again and decide whether the following statements are true (T) or false (F).

(1) The objective of a post-show evaluation is only to know which employee works best in the show. ( )
(2) While doing a show evaluation, we should measure the effect of the trade show against the initial objectives. ( )
(3) If you keep good records of post-show evaluations, you will do better in the next show. ( )
(4) Most show exhibitors do not follow up after the show. ( )
(5) Do not take it for granted that people you met at the trade show will call you. ( )
(6) It is better to follow up with all the leads within 24 hours of the show. ( )
(7) It is unnecessary to e-mail all the booth visitors available. ( )
(8) We should only contact those attendees with good prospects. ( )

2. Translate the following sentences using as many language skills learnt in this lesson as possible.

(1) 人们常常忽略展后评估和会展后续工作。
(2) 如果您有这样的习惯，您将能够预测下一个展览会的效果。
(3) 参展后，你应该思考你从别人那里学到了什么。
(4) 您回到办公室后，您不应该立刻着手新的项目。
(5) 你应该给所有留下联系方式的参展人员发送电邮。

Section Ⅳ The Internet Research

1. Research after class through the Internet to look for tips on how to evaluate the results after the show.
2. Get information of one product and be ready for dialogue practice next class.
Take down the following information about the product:
Product Name;
Factory Location;
Product Features;

Minimum Quantity;
Price;
Requirement;
Sales Office/Representative Office.
Suggested website: http://www.tdctrade.com.

Section V   New Words You've Met in This Lesson

recommend	vt.	推荐
appoint	vt.	指派
client	n.	客户
dismantle	vt.	拆除
strengthen	vt.	加强
evaluation	n.	评估
overflowing	adj.	溢流的，过剩的
multiple	adj.	多层次的，多项的
categorize	vt.	分类，使……归类
lead	n.	领导，榜样
preserve	vt.	保留，预留
evaluate	vt.	评估，估计
obtain	vt.	获得，得到
measure	vt.	测量，估量
imperative	adj.	紧急的，必要的
initial	adj.	最初的

Section VI   Writing Related to EC Industry

Write a notice on behalf of the organizing committee of the High-tech Exhibition to inform all the exhibitors that the exhibition will be lengthened one more day. The closing ceremony will be on September 12 and move-out on September 13~15.

A model of notice is given in the following.

[Model]

Dismantling Notice

All exhibitors:

　　The exhibition center will be closed and the power will be turned off at 21:30 on October 2, 2008. For security reasons no one will be allowed to remain in the hall after this time.

The exhibition center will re-open the following day for staff with exhibitor passes to start removing their stands, display materials and exhibits from 09:00 on October 3, 2008.

All stands, display materials, and exhibits must be removed by 19:00 on October 5, 2008.

It is the responsibility of each exhibitor to be at his stand during the dismantling to see the removing of his exhibits.

Organizing Committee
September 29, 2008

Notice

All exhibitors:

_____

_____

Section VII Review of This Unit

1. Jargons in This Unit

cancellation money	解约金
lost profit	利润损失
costs incurred on behalf of sb.	由某人引起的费用
registration number	预定号
termination clause	解约条款
forfeit deposit	没收押金
nonrefundable	不可退还的
display item	展品

续表

move-out	撤展
transportation company	运输公司
exhibition manual	参展手册
storage area	存储区

2. Sentence Patterns/Practical Dialogues

1) Canceling a reservation

(1) I am calling to call off a trade show registration.

(2) I am informing you of my inability to take part in the exhibition.

(3) I want to know how to cancel the registration.

(4) Please tell me the exact amount of money I can get back from the exhibit organizer, if I withdraw from it now.

(5) Would you please tell me the minimum time of advancing a canceling notice?

2) Revise a reservation

(1) I am calling to revise my registration for the exhibition.

(2) Could you please tell me whether there are vacant booths for the exhibition? I want to reserve two more booths.

3. Writing Related to EC Industry

Write a notice on behalf of the organizing committee of a fair.

Unit 6

Post-Conference Tour
会 后 游

> 单元目标

1. 认识会展服务公司除了策划会展项目、布置会展展台等工作外,还需要为客户策划合理的会后旅游路线。
2. 了解本地风景名胜,能熟练运用英语与客户商讨会后游的相关问题。
3. 学会书写旅游路线。
4. 进一步学习组织会后游的策略及目的。

Section Ⅰ A Sample Dialogue

[Scene] Mr. Smith, client, is talking with Xu Hui, an exhibition strategist with the Kebo Exhibition about the post-conference tour for attendees of the exhibition.

客户史密斯先生正在与科博会展服务公司的会展策划师徐惠商讨会后旅游事宜。

Xu Hui: Good afternoon, Mr. Smith! I have been expecting you.
Smith: Good afternoon, Miss Xu! Sorry for keeping you waiting.
Xu Hui: That's all right. Let's get down to work.
Smith: Okay. I would like to discuss with you about one ideal itinerary of the post-conference tour for the attendees.
Xu Hui: May I ask for your requirements for this tour?
Smith: That tour should take less than 2 days. I would like to have the itinerary include scenic spots of typical features of Chongqing.
Xu Hui: I have already collected some useful information and checked with the travel agency. I hope my suggestions will be helpful. I'd like to recommend some places of interest for your reference.
Smith: Okay, let's go over them.
Xu Hui: I highly recommend Ciqikou, a small town conveying the impression of Chongqing of the distant past and Hongyadong, a newly-built structure, which maintains the traditional architectural style of Chongqing and integrates a great variety of delicious local foods there.
Smith: Good. These two places should be put on the list.
Xu Hui: What's more, we can also put the Nanshan Mountain, the Jiefangbei shopping area in the list.
Smith: Yes. The attendees can climb the mountain and then return to the shopping area to buy some presents for their family members and friends. How thoughtful!
Xu Hui: For a two-day tour, we can also organize the attendees to leave the city center and go to have a cruise on the Yangtze River. They can visit the Three Gorges.
Smith: I'm not so sure. It seems that the cruise is costly and time-consuming. Let me think it over.
Xu Hui: All right. Maybe we should focus on the city tour. This itinerary covers all famous places within the city and takes less time.
Smith: I can't agree with you more.
Xu Hui: As we reach an agreement on the tour, I shall contact the travel agency to make a reservation of the post-conference tour and confirm the itinerary with the tour guide.
Smith: Okay, that's it. Thank you for your time and consideration. Let's keep in touch.
Xu Hui: Okay. If there is any problem, don't hesitate to let me know.

Smith: I won't. Goodbye!

Xu Hui: Goodbye!

(Xu Hui is calling the travel agency to reserve a one-day post-conference city tour.)

Clerk: Good morning. May I help you?

Xu Hui: Yes. I would like to book a one-day city tour for my group.

Clerk: How many is it for?

Xu Hui: 66.

Clerk: In your case, you need two coaches. When would you like to go?

Xu Hui: Next Monday, when the convention comes to its end.

Clerk: Do you need a guide to serve your group throughout the tour?

Xu Hui: Certainly. The guide is required to speak both English and Mandarin fluently.

Clerk: No problem. But we will have to charge more in your case.

Xu Hui: How much does it cost?

Clerk: ¥150 per person.

Xu Hui: Okay. May I see the itinerary? Maybe I would like to make some changes to it personally.

Clerk: Okay. May I have your email address please? I would like to send it to you right away.

Xu Hui: That's good. My E-mail account is keboxuhui@126.com.

Clerk: OK, I got it. If you want to make any change to the original itinerary, please contact me as soon as possible. And our tour guide will confirm with you the itinerary and timetable of the tour.

Xu Hui: Thank you very much.

1. Read the conversation again and decide whether the following statements are true (T) or false (F).

(1) Smith prefers a post-conference tour lasting more than 2 days. ( )

(2) The attendees will have a chance to visit the beautiful Three Gorges. ( )

(3) Xu Hui wants to hire a bilingual tour guide who speaks both Chinese and English. ( )

(4) The tour will cost ¥6,600 totally. ( )

(5) The clerk at the travel agency will send a copy of the itinerary by fax to Xu Hui. ( )

(6) Xu may make some changes to the original itinerary. ( )

(7) The group will focus on the city tour, that is to say, they will not travel to other places outside the city. ( )

(8) Smith is quite happy with the introduction of a shopping area, because the attendees can have a chance to buy local presents for family members and friends. ( )

2. Discuss with your partner the local scenic spots which are suitable for post-conference travel programs in your city and summarize ways of planning post-conference trips.

3. Match the jargons on the left with the Chinese equivalents on the right.

(1) post-conference tour   a. 变更，修改

(2) souvenir b. 包价旅游
(3) exhibition strategist c. 旅行社
(4) itinerary d. 会后旅游
(5) package tour e. 名胜
(6) travel agency f. 旅行路线
(7) one-day city sightseeing g. 纪念品
(8) places of interests h. 会展策划师
(9) destination i. 市内一日观光游
(10) make alterations to j. 目的地

Section Ⅱ Communication Activities

1. Pair Work

The following chart is about the routes of an post-conference tour. The 3 routes are provided by the EnerEnv' 2003 conference. Please read through the chart and work with a partner. Take turns to introduce different routes to each other.

Routes	Duration	Brief introduction	Cost
The Zhangjiajie National Park	4 days/3 nights	Zhangjiajie municipality is a place that has extraordinary sight in the northwest of Hunan Province. It is the first national forest park in China, also famous both in China and aboard. It lies in the Wuling Mountains, 32km away from Zhangjiajie city proper. It consists of the Zhangjiajie National Forest Park, the Tianzi Mountain, the Suoxi Valley, and Yangjiajie, each with a unique landscape.	$350 per person
Chengdu-Jiuzhaigou -Dujiangyan	5 days/5 nights	Jiuzhaigou is a National Park and UNESCO World Heritage site. It is located in northern Sichuan, and it is often called a fairyland by the Chinese because of its beauty. The name Jiuzhaigou came from nine Tibetan villages scattered around in the valley. Its attraction lies in a simple beauty: a fairyland, primitive and natural, without a single drop of dirt. Here you can find majestic emerald lakes, layer upon layer of waterfalls, colorful forests, and snow peaks.	$600 per person
Kunming-Dali- Shangrila	6 days/5 nights	Shangrila, a beautiful and strange name, is synonymous with the Garden of Eden(伊甸园). In the year 1933, James Hilton described an eternally peaceful and quiet place among mountains in the East—"Shangrila" in one of his novels with the name of "Lost Horizon".	$850 per person

2. Role Play

Please work in a group of three and make a conversation, following the process of the EnerEnv' 2003 Conference.

Student A & B: attendees of the conference

Student C: the convention organizer of the conference

[Sample dialogue]

A & B: Hi, Mr. C. We are here for some information about the post-conference tour.

C: We've prepared three routes for you to choose.

A: Would you please elaborate on them?

C: Sure!

B: Thank you.

C: You're welcome.

[Useful expressions]

Attendees	Organizer
We're interested in the trip to Jiuzhaigou. May I ask how long the trip takes?	If you could afford time, do visit it!
What's special about this scenic spot?	You will have a chance to feast your eyes on the marvelous relics of Chinese civilization.
May I ask for the price of this trip?	It's rather costly. You have to spend … on it. But you will find it to be worthwhile later.
Would you please introduce to us places of sightseeing within the Zhangjiajie scenic spot?	You will have a chance to go to the Suoxi Valley in Zhangjiajie.

Section Ⅲ Expansion Reading

[导读]

该文来自CONASTA (The Conference of the Australian Science Teachers Association,澳大利亚理科教师联盟会议)58。该会已于2009年7月4—7日召开,在会议之前,会议组织方将会后旅游路线发布到网上供与会人员挑选。由于该会在澳大利亚塔斯马尼亚州召开,因此会后旅游也集中在该地区。

CONASTA 58 Post Conference Tour

Wednesday 8 July – Friday 10 July, 2009

Tasmanian World Heritage Area: Cradle Mountain

Aim of the Conference: To highlight the Tasmanian Wilderness World Heritage area, its values and importance and to gain first-hand experience of the research and conservation programs being undertaken in this area.

The Tasmanian Wilderness World Heritage Area protects one of the last true wilderness regions on earth, and includes a greater range of natural and cultural values than any other region. It covers about 1.38 million hectares and covers about one fifth of the area of Tasmania. The area is formally recognized through its World Heritage listing (1982) on the basis of all four natural criteria and three cultural criteria. It has satisfied more criteria than any other World Heritage property.

Unit 6 Post-Conference Tour 会后游

Following CONASTA 58, you are invited to participate in the Cradle Mountain Post Conference tour spending three days and two nights in the Tasmanian World Heritage Area.

Proposed Itinerary

Wednesday 8 July

8:00 am: Departure from Launceston and travel to Cradle Mountain via Mole Creek Karst national Park

10:00 am: Marakoopa Cave Tour (Light morning tea provided)

The Mole Creek area contains over 300 known caves. Other typical karst features in this area include gorges and large underground streams and springs. These caves are home to a number of interesting animals. The glow-worm display in Marakoopa Cave is the largest you'll see in any other cave in Australia. If Weather permits, there'll be the opportunity to take a short walk through the beautiful forests in which these caves are located.

11:30 am: Leaving Mole Creek National Park and travel to Cradle Mountain

12:30 pm: Arriving Cradle Mountain and lunch

2:00 pm: Introductory session at Visitor Centre with PWS staff and rainforest walk

The vegetation of the Cradle Mountain area is made up of a diverse range of vegetation communities from rainforest to grassland. This walk will introduce you to the ancient plants.

3:30 pm: Afternoon tea and accommodation at Cradle Mountain Lodge; free time to explore Lodge surrounds.

5:00 pm: Devils at Cradle Tour

6:30 pm: Dinner at Lodge Tavern

Evening: Slide presentation of flora of Cradle Mountain

Thursday 9 July

8:00 am: Breakfast

9:00 am: Morning sessions—guided walks

Dove Lake and Waldheim (includes morning tea)

Dove Lake is a 2km long glacial lake situated at the base of Cradle Mountain. There is a 7.5km walk around the lake which is probably one of the most popular wilderness walks in

Tasmania. It is a relatively easy walk on a raised boardwalk, taking about 2 hours to complete. Along the way there are wonderful views of Cradle Mountain and a variety of native plants and animals.

12:30 pm: Lunch at Cradle Mt. Lodge

2:00 pm: Afternoon sessions—talks and workshops

(1) Research presentations on topics such as threatened species research and conservation, and World Heritage Area management.

(2) Parks & wildlife education programs for schools.

5:00 pm: Free time

6:30 pm: Dinner at Highland Restaurant

Evening: Night wildlife tour with PWS staff

Friday 10 July

8:00 am: Breakfast and free time to take advantage of Lodge facilities and other short walks nearby

10:00 am: Departure from Cradle Mountain and return to Launceston via Devonport

11:30 am: Visit to a science centre in Devonport

12:30 pm: Lunch at House of Anvers—including a short tour of a chocolate factory

4:00 pm: Arriving Launceston

Points To Note

(1) At this time of year, it will be cold at Cradle Mountain (average monthly temperature is 5~6℃), snow is possible, and warm clothing is essential. Waterproof coats, woolen hats and gloves, and good walking shoes are recommended.

(2) Activities will be weather dependent, so be prepared for flexibility in the schedule.

(3) The trip is not available for children ; partners of science teachers are welcome to attend and may join in all activities.

Cost

Total cost (based on twin share accommodation): $690.00 per person.

Extra cost single room supplement ($190): $880.00 per person.

Payments: $200 deposit due March 1, 2009

Final payment due May 1, 2009 (all payments to Conference Design).

1. Answer the following questions orally according to the passage.

(1) Where will attendees of the conference go for their post-conference tour?

(2) What is the aim of the tour?

(3) How long will the trip last?

(4) How much will the tour cost per person?

(5) If you take part in the tour, what should you take along with to the tourist destination?

(6) Who are not encouraged to take part in the tour and who are welcome?

(7) If you want to join in the tour, how much should you pay as a deposit?

(8) After reading the passage, what do you think are the purposes of post-conference tours?

2. Translate the following sentences using as many language skills learned in this lesson as possible.

(1) 7月8日下午3点半之后是大家自由活动的时间。

(2) 此景点是典型的喀斯特地貌。你将欣赏到壮美的峡谷和瑰丽的洞穴。

(3) 晚餐后请各位参加一个研讨会议，探讨保护区内濒危物种的保护问题，以及保护区的管理事宜。

(4) 天气变化会导致旅游路线的变化，因此请随时为路线变更做好准备。

(5) A：早上好！我有什么可以帮您的？

B：我想了解一下市内一日观光游的信息。来这座城市之前，我听说它是一座很有特色的城市。

A：这是一座旅游资源丰富的城市。我们旅行社能为您量身定做一条市内一日游路线。

B：太好了，我能来贵社看看路线吗？我们团人数比较多，众口难调。

A：当然可以。我们旅行社一定可以为贵团打造一条令人满意的旅游路线。由于贵团人数较多，我建议您考虑包价旅游。

B：好的。我下午来旅行社拿旅游信息册子，以及商量旅游路线问题。

A：好的。到时候见！

B：再见！

Section Ⅳ The Internet Research

1. Search for information about 2 important tourist attractions in your city, or the city you're familiar with. Write down the brief introduction to them.

2. Find on-line the types and purposes of post-conference tours.

3. Surf the Net for the tendency and strategies of the development of post-conference tours.

Section Ⅴ New Words You've Met in This Unit

integrate	v.	整合
time-consuming	adj.	浪费时间的
reservation	n.	预订
landscape	n.	地貌，风景
heritage	n.	遗产
fairyland	n.	仙境
synonymous	adj.	同义的
flora	n.	植物群

续表

wilderness	n.	荒野
underground stream	n.	地下河
glow-worm	n.	萤火虫
session	n.	开庭，开会
workshop	n.	专题讨论会，讲习班
vegetation	n.	植物，草木
creek	n.	小湾，小溪
diverse	adj.	多样的
boardwalk	n.	木板路

Section Ⅵ Writing Related to EC Industry

1. When you have decided where to go and what to see, it's time to write your itinerary. This itinerary will record the details of your trip from your departure time until when you go back home. It is recommended that you use a chart or a table.

[Sample]

Proposed Itinerary

Wednesday, 1 June

9:00 am: Departure from hotel and travel to the Gele Mountain

10:00 am: Visit the Zhazidong Prison

This is the most famous prison set up by the conspired Kuomingdang and its American supporters during the Civil War period of China. It was once a coal mine and is located at the foot of the Gele Mountain. Shortly before the founding of the PRC, prisoners, mostly Chinese communists, were slaughtered by the henchmen(党羽，跟随者) of Jiangjieshi, the head of Kuomingdang. In the very location one can imagine those who sacrificed their life for the welfare of the Chinese nation.

11:00 am: Go to Ciqikou

Ciqikou is a town conveying the impression of Chongqing of the distant past. It is situated on the bank of the Jia Ling River, not far from its confluence with the mighty Yangtze. It is the ancient village of Ciqikou, formerly known as Long Yin. During the Ming and Qing Dynasties (1368-1911) it was famous for its production of porcelain. In the ancient town Ciqikou, you can ramble(漫步) on the traditional street paved with flagstones to the ancient wharf. There you can imagine the prosperity of the shipping industry in the past.

12:00 am: Lunch at a local restaurant

1:30 pm: Travel to Jiefangbei—the shopping area of Chongqing

2:30 pm: Meeting with organizers of the Shopping Carnival in Chongqing

4:00 pm: Free time to go shopping

5:30 pm: Travel to Hongyadong and dinner at a five-star restaurant

7:00 pm: Return to hotel

2. Write an itinerary according to the information given.

Design an itinerary of a one-day trip in your city.

Section Ⅶ Review of This Unit

1. Jargons in This Unit

post-conference tour	会后游
souvenir	纪念品
exhibition strategist	会展策划师
itinerary	旅游路线
package tour	包价旅游
coach	旅游大巴
one-day city sightseeing	市内一日观光游
places of interest	名胜
destination	目的地
make alternations to	修改，变更
route	路线
make a reservation	预定

2. Sentence Patterns/Practical Dialogues

(1) May I ask for your requirements of the post-conference tour?

(2) The tour should take less than … days. I'd like to have the itinerary include scenic spots of typical features of … city.

(3) I would like to book a one-day city tour for my group.

(4) How many is it for?

(5) In your case, you need two limousine buses. When would you like to go?

(6) Do you need a guide to serve your group throughout the tour?

(7) Have you made any alteration to the itinerary?

(8) Hardly any change at all.

(9) May I ask how long the tour lasts?

(10) It takes … days and … nights.

(11) What's special about the scenic spot?

(12) There are many beautiful lakes there. You'll have a good chance to feast your eyes on these lakes.

3. Writing Related to EC Industry

Write an itinerary of a tour.

Unit 7

Exhibition and Conference Strategies

会 展 策 略

单元目标

1. 区分组展商和参展商的不同利益、不同工作性质和责任。
2. 从组展商的角度看会展策略,了解成功的会展表现。
3. 从参展商的角度看会展策略,了解如何从参展中获益。

Unit 7 Exhibition and Conference Strategies 会展策略

Lesson 1

Organizers' Strategies
组展方的策略

Section I A Sample Dialogue

[Scene] *City Business Newspaper* reports that in October. 2008, 50 exhibitors who attended the International Luxury Goods Exhibition held at the International Exhibition and Conference Center sued the exhibition organizer, because they felt cheated. This exhibition has aroused a lot of public talk and thinking about the duty of exhibition organizers. A group of local residents are now talking about it.

《都市商报》报道了 2008 年 10 月 "国际奢侈品展 50 参展商欲告主办方",因为他们觉得被 "水" 了。市民们关于这场展会的谈论和思考还没有结束。

Resident A: Have you read yesterday's *Evening Newspaper*?
Resident B: I know what you are going to talk about. Is it about the exhibition? It has become the biggest and hottest local news already.
Resident A: You know it?
Resident B: I visited the exhibition myself yesterday and I felt cheated to a certain degree.
Resident C: What happened there?
Resident B: In their advertisement, the corporate organizer, Meisha Exhibition Company from Shenzhen, boasted that private jets, sofa with diamonds, and a lot of world-famous top luxury brands would be on display at the exhibition. A lot of visitors and I paid ¥50 for entrance tickets to get in. But to our extreme disappointment, we didn't find any world-famous top luxury brands at all, but rather exhibits from domestic exhibitors. Most of them are jade products, roots sculptures, jewelry, and paintings. Nothing special.
Resident A: The newspaper reported exactly the same thing. What's more, the prices of the exhibits vary so much that the visitors feel uncomfortable. The highest price is ¥36 million for a jade vase, while the lowest is ¥10 for a jade imitation bracelet. How can a bracelet costing ¥10, which can be seen anywhere on a roadside ornament stand, be called luxury goods?
Resident C: Has any rich man appeared in the center? Is it a good chance to see celebrities who are nowhere to be seen except on these occasions?
Resident A: There was nobody! The Newspaper says that not a single local wealthy man

Resident A: has stepped in, not to mention those from other richer places, such as Shanghai or Beijing.

Resident B: You two are lucky not to have been there.

Resident A: The news tells that the organizer's excuse for not having a satisfactory exhibition is the massive earthquake that took place not long ago and not far from our city. They have not made any profit from it. What's worse, there might even be a court case because the organizer failed to return the 20% deposit to 50 exhibitors in order to compensate their losses as it promised. Now the exhibitors feel so cheated and annoyed that they may sue the organizer.

Resident C: What a shame! Has the organizer ever thought about the practicality of holding a luxury goods exhibition in an inland city, like Chongqing? People's average monthly income is no more than ¥2,200 ! A lot of factors need to be considered before organizing an exhibition this size.

Resident A and B: You are absolutely right.

1. Read the conversation again and decide whether the following statements are true (T) or false (F).

(1) The organizer of this luxury goods exhibition is a corporate organization, not a governmental one. ( )

(2) The exhibition has aroused a lot of public interest and dispute because it failed to keep its promises. ( )

(3) In inland cities, such as Chongqing, in which the average monthly salary is no more than ¥2,200, better planning is demanded than in bigger cities when organizing luxury goods exhibitions. ( )

(4) None of the exhibition parties (exhibitors, organizers, and visitors) are satisfied with the results of the exhibition. ( )

(5) Some local celebrities turned up in the show, so visitors had the chance to see them closely. ( )

(6) The massive earthquake that took place 1 month before the exhibition in a nearby place had a huge influence on the exhibition. ( )

(7) 50 exhibitors have sued the organizer for not returning the deposits to them. ( )

(8) Exhibition organizers have to take a lot of factors into consideration when preparing for shows. ( )

2. Discuss in groups and fill in the chart.

Exhibition organizers (EOs) are either corporate organizations or governmental organizations. But in China the role of an organizer is often played by government offices and authority departments. For example, the organizers of the 2008 China Chongqing Tea Expo were Chongqing City Commercial Committee & the Chongqing City Commercial Federation. There are even quite a few co-organizers, such as the Chongqing Municipal Agricultural Bureau of Agricultural

Unit 7　Exhibition and Conference Strategies 会展策略

Sciences, the Yunnan tea Chamber of Commerce of Chongqing Municipality, and the Tea Industry Association of Zhejiang Province. Fortunately, now the routine is under change. Many professional exhibition companies are appearing to undertake the task of organizing exhibitions.

However, in western countries most EOs are professional companies rather than government organizations. Discuss with 4 partners what factors have caused this difference, and what advantages and disadvantages each system has (Chinese organization system or western system).

Countries	Possible reasons for the difference	Advantages	Disadvantages
China			
Western			

3. Match the jargons on the left with the Chinese equivalents on the right.

(1) luxury goods　　　　　　　　　　a. 参展
(2) domestic exhibitor　　　　　　　　b. 营销策略
(3) deposit　　　　　　　　　　　　　c. 直邮
(4) participation　　　　　　　　　　 d. 奢侈品
(5) visitor promotion　　　　　　　　 e. 定金/押金
(6) marketing strategy　　　　　　　　f. 小册子
(7) direct mail　　　　　　　　　　　 g. 国内参展商
(8) brochure　　　　　　　　　　　　 h. 国外参展商
(9) overseas exhibitor　　　　　　　　i. 赞助商
(10) sponsor　　　　　　　　　　　　 j. 吸引观众

Section Ⅱ　Communication Activities

1. Pair Work

Work in pairs and discuss the strategies adopted by the exhibition organizer and their purposes. Try to complete the following chart. (There's no fixed answer to the question in the chart.)

Party	Strategies	Purposes
Exhibition Organizers	choosing a first-tier city as the location of the exhibition	…
	…	to satisfy customers
	…	to impress show visitors
	choosing the well-renowned sponsors	…

2. Role Play

Make conversations following the sample.

Student A: Exhibition strategist A
Student B: Exhibition strategist B

[Sample dialogue]

A: Our company will organize the 2009 International Automobile Exhibition. This is a big event and our company aims at making money from it. We have to think about different strategies to make the exhibition wonderful and attractive.

B: You're right. As the two of us are entrusted with the task of pre-exhibition planning, we have to work hard on it. Any suggestions?

A: I think we should decide upon the location of the exhibition first.

B: Uh, as for the location, I highly recommend Shanghai. In this big event, BMW, BUICK, Ford, Daimler-Benz will send their new models to our exhibition. They would like to meet potential buyers.

A: Yes. The targeted customers of these new models are the rich in our country. After analyzing the purchasing power, I think Shanghai should be one of the more suitable locations for our exhibition. But how about Guangzhou, also among the first-tier cities in our country?

B: Yeah, there are a lot of entrepreneurs(企业家) living in Guangzhou and Shenzhen. They are also potential buyers.

A: We have to do some research into the markets of the two cities. After we get the statistics, we can make a final decision.

B: That's right. We should contact the department of research immediately to ask them to get down to work.

A: Okay, I'll make the call.

[Situation 1] The two discuss using direct mail or other means to invite potential buyers.

[Situation 2] The two discuss inviting famous trans-national companies or governmental organizations as the sponsors of the exhibition.

[Situation 3] The two discuss how to accommodate top branded exhibitors in this exhibition, aiming to achieve the industry credibility.

Section Ⅲ Expansion Reading

[导读]

组展商要做的工作是整体的、全局的，和个体的参展商有很大差异。他们的战略战术也有一定的特殊性和挑战性。

Exhibition Organizer's Performance Strategies

Much of the exhibitors' work has little in common with the exhibition organizer's (EO), since the former focuses on individual exhibitor performance, while an organizer is concerned with collective exhibitor performance. For example, the location and the size of the booth for an exhibitor is a major concern for success in exhibition participation. The EO, on the other hand, is more concerned with the location of the whole exhibition (which city) and the overall visitor promotion and attraction.

Unit 7　Exhibition and Conference Strategies 会展策略

Everyone has his own idea about the basic elements of a successful show, such as servicing the exhibitors and boosting the number of attendees. The most important things an exhibition management operation could do are to satisfy customers, provide employees with jobs, and make money. To make customers and workers happy, a money-making business is a must. To achieve these the exhibition organizer has to make use of many strategies.

(1) Planning: Planning with short and long-range goals and objectives was important.

(2) Intelligence gathering and analysis is critical to exhibit sales in today's increasingly competitive show environment.

(3) Branding provides another competitive advantage. An exhibition must be large in scale and include all the top branded exhibitors in its market.

(4) Publication: Trade magazine publishers bring a unique business to business (B2B) perspective from publishing. The leading multi-national EOs (such as REED and CMP) and the leading Hong Kong-based EOs (such as Adsale, Info Communication, Global Service, Sinostar and Business/Industry (B&I) all have trade publications related to their trade exhibitions. EOs use publishing strategies to promote their exhibitions to:

(a) Gain industry credibility and build loyalty. Publication editors have strong visibility in the industry.

(b) Know their audience. Publications have to show value in every issue.

(c) Prove their value. Magazine content could be a model for show content. Magazines focus on the buyers, and the suppliers follow.

(5) Direct mailing and IT, and other technology factors bring benefits to attendee promotion, online marketing, and telemarketing.

Direct mail is the lifeblood of trade show promotion. It is efficient, low cost, and measurable. According to Trade Show Bureau research, 81% of show managers use direct mail as their primary means of attracting attendees. Typically, 38% of their attendees are attracted through direct mail. On average, show organizers spend 64% of the promotion budget in direct marketing (lists, emails, brochures, postcards, printing, postage, etc.).

(6) Taking advantage of international agents: American EOs have not been active internationally or in China for outbound and inbound exhibitions. International agents are recommended to attract overseas exhibitors. An international agent's most immediate advantage is an existing command of the language and business customs of the target market.

(7) Highlighting the role of sponsors: Quality of attendees is more attractive than quantity. Another marketing skill is involved in forming the exhibition sponsors. The functions of sponsors are not to be overlooked. In China it is imperative to seek help and fund from governmental organizations, trade associations, media, and other relevant units in this country. It helps promote the reputation and authoritative influence of the exhibition.

1. Answer the following questions orally according to the passage.

(1) Why is organizers' job different from that of exhibitors?

(2) What work does the public think EOs should do?

(3) What strategies can EOs use according to the text?

(4) What means do EOs use to spread knowledge about an upcoming important exhibition or conference?

(5) What does "branding" mean in the text?

(6) Why is direct mailing an effective way to spread awareness about exhibition?

(7) What is the role of international agents?

(8) What is the function of sponsors?

2. Translate the following sentences using as many language skills learned in this lesson as possible.

(1) 出席本次展会的参展商要控告主办方。

(2) 主办方若未能实现承诺，则退还15%的定金给参展商。

(3) 组展商注重所有的参展商的表现，而个体参展商则更多的是关心自己的展会位置面积等。

(4) 主办方可以利用许多营销手段来招商，如打出会展场所的知名度，做广告，甚至利用国际会展代理商。

(5) 赞助商功不可没，它能吸引高质量的参展商和观众。

Section Ⅳ   The Internet Research

1. What are the major preparations that exhibition organizers are required to do before the opening of an exhibition?

2. What is the history of the International Luxury Exhibition?

3. How long has the luxury exhibition been in existence in China?

Section Ⅴ   New Words You've Met in This Lesson

advertisement	n.	广告
corporate	adj.	公司的
compensate	vt.	补偿，赔偿
average	adj.	平均的
celebrity	n.	知名人士，名人
individual	adj.	个别的，单独的，个人的
concerned with/about	adj.	关切的；有关（方面）的，忧虑的
overall	adj.	全面的；综合的
boost	v.	加强，增加；促进；提高；支援
long-range	adj.	远程的，远大的，长期的
brand	v.	使……显得突出；使永志难忘；铭记

Unit 7 Exhibition and Conference Strategies 会展策略

续表

perspective	n.	眼界，洞察力，观点，看法
multi-national	adj.	多民族(国家)的；多(跨)国公司的
credibility	n.	可靠性，可信性
kit	n.	成套用品，配套元件

Lesson 2

Exhibitors' Strategies
参展商的策略

Section I A Sample Dialogue

[Scene] Shuangwei Air Nailer Company Ltd. has made a decision to participate in an international tools exhibition in Germany. The sales manager is concerned with the exhibition strategy and style. Now he is having a meeting with his staff.

双伟钉枪有限公司决定参加在德国举行的一次国际展览。销售经理为公司的展览策略和风格非常操心。他正在和员工开会。

Manager: Good morning. We are having a brief meeting here. By the end of the meeting, we need to determine the strategy and style of our exhibition.

Staff A: Exhibition strategy and style go hand-in-hand with each other. We need to consider them both.

Staff B: Our exhibition performance focuses on selling goods, including those on exposure to exhibits, booth contacts, overall sales, and awareness of new products. Thus our tactical and strategic recommendation is to improve the use of exhibitions during new product introductions, and the motivation behind exhibition participation.

Manager: You are aware of the emergence and theory of exhibition. So what practical suggestions do you have?

Staff A: We must do well in the following steps. First, plan and prepare well. Second, perform well at the exhibition. And finally, assess effectively and follow up closely after the exhibition.

Manager: Clear suggestions. Thanks. (turning to staff B) Well, what would you like to propose?

Staff B: I think we should make specific arrangements under every step proposed by A. For example, when we are planning and preparing, we'd better set down exhibition goals. For example, what are our primary goals and secondary goals? Is it to raise visitors' awareness of our new products? Or is it to meet and further our communication with all the existing customers?

Manager: Marvellous ideas! You two know well what is to be done before the participation of the exhibition. But it's a pity that it seems we cannot make a decision in today's 30-minute meeting. In 3 days I'd like the two of you work out an exhibition strategy plan together and hand it in to me. And we are going to have another 30-minute meeting to look at your proposals.

Staff A & B: OK, no problem.

1. Answer the following questions orally according to the conversation.

(1) Why is the manager worried?

(2) What is the major issue discussed at the meeting?

(3) What does staff A mean by "strategy and style go hand-in-hand with each other"?

(4) What are the company's aims in participating in this exhibition?

(5) According to staff A, there are 3 steps the exhibitor must follow in order to succeed in an exhibition. What are these steps?

(6) Does staff B agree with staff A's suggestion? What is staff B's proposal?

(7) What assignment does the manager give to the staff members?

(8) Is the meeting successful?

2. In groups, sum up the aspects to consider in order to have unique exhibition style. The concept of exhibition styles provides a guideline from which the design elements of a booth can be chosen and the marketing instruments can be selected. (参展风格指导着展台的设计, 以及营销/促销手段的选择。有哪些因素可以决定参展风格呢?)

[For example]

The management has to choose which communication instruments (i.e. press conference, brochure, direct mailing, special event, banners, advertisement) to use. The following chart can help you to consider the aspects of styles.

Communication instruments	Booth decoration	Staff	Products demonstration	Marketing
e.g. press conference,	e.g. color	e.g. uniform	e.g. hand-outs	e.g. advertisement

3. Match the jargons on the left with the Chinese equivalents on the right.

(1) exhibition strategy and style   a. 总的销售量

(2) exhibition performance   b. 展品曝光率/展品宣传

(3) exhibits exposure   c. 参展表现

(4) booth contacts   d. 参展策略和风格

(5) overall sales   e. 后续/后期跟进

(6) awareness of new product   f. 展台签约/展台合同

(7) product introduction   g. 认识新产品

(8) follow-up   h. 发放品

(9) existing and potential customers   i. 产品推介

Unit 7 Exhibition and Conference Strategies 会展策略

(10) hand-out   j. 现有和潜在的客户

Section II Communication Activities

1．Role Play

Getting the most out of the staff during the show is an essential skill. Now try to motivate a staff member in the following situations. You are an exhibitor.

[Sample dialogue]

You: What's wrong, Miss Lee? You look unwell.
Lee: I didn't sleep well last night because I am not used to sleeping in a hotel.
You: Have a seat at the table and have some tea.

(A while later)

You: Do you feel better now? You've performed wonderfully until now. I hope you can carry it on until the end of the day.
Lee: Thanks for the encouragement. I'll do my best.

[Situations]

Wang	Nancy	Judy	Candy
hurt, high-heel shoes	nervous, have no idea how to communicate with strangers	exhausted after standing for half a day	lost voice after talking with visitors

2. Role Play

You are a sales manager who is to set goals for a show. After the show, you will also assess the achievements with the staff.

Goals set: To expose new products to visitors, chiefly strangers;
                  To meet 25 qualified new prospects ;
                  To acquaint the existing customers with new products;
                  To sell products on spot.

Assessment: De-brief the team (thanks, praise for the efforts, expectations).

Sum up what worked and what didn't. (e.g. better arrangement of display exhibits; eye-catching uniforms of staff members; labor service ordered in advance).

Discuss suggestions for improving performance at future exhibitions. (Stick to specific business goals; decide which visitors are the right-fit.)

Follow up all contacts: Timely letter, e-mail.

[Sample dialogue]

(Before the show)

Manager: Then you know what goals we are to achieve at the show?
Wang: Yes, we are to sell 300 sewing machines on the spot.
Lee: If possible, we are to sign at least double-value contracts of last year.

(One day after they got back from the show)

Manager:	Dear team, you performed wonderfully during the show. I'd like to give you my heart-felt thanks for your efforts and cooperation. Do you know what we are going to do next?
Lee:	We are to contact those who came to visit our stand.
Manager:	Yes, you are right. That's exactly what we are going to do next. But before that, let's sum up what has worked well during the show.
Wang:	We set up specific goals in advance, and we reached the goals in the end.
Manager:	I think so, too. Then have you realized what didn't work well?
Lee:	If our exhibition theme had been more eye-catching, we would have attracted more visitors. Some of them told me that they didn't realize our products would turn out to be so satisfying. They were not attracted by the posters on our booth. They happened to walk inside. And they were overjoyed with the unexpected findings of our products.
Manager:	Really? If so, that's what we are to work on at future exhibitions. By the way, do you know how to contact those who came to visit our booth?
Wang:	Every visitor to our exhibition stand should receive a timely follow-up. We can send them a simple thank-you letter, information pack, e-mail, or give them a phone call.

Section Ⅲ Expansion Reading

[导读]

成百上千的同行业参展商齐聚一堂，竞争激烈可想而知。那么怎么样才能"万花丛中一点绿"呢？三个阶段的战略战术就得派上用场了。

Strategies to Ensure Your Sales Leads at Exhibitions

Exhibitions allow your company to interact with your target audience face-to-face in a very specific environment. How do you stand out? The following suggestions will help you.

1. Plan and Prepare

(1) Set Specific Goals

The more specific and realistic your goals, the more likely you will achieve them. But, make sure you dig deeper when identifying your prospects.

Do you want to acquaint the existing customers with new products, or to sell products on the spot?

(2) Prepare Your Exhibition Staff

The staff needs to understand the specific goals of the event, potential questions that may arise from a visitor and whom to target. Remind them of the strengths and weaknesses of the team, as well as of the products. If you motivate your staff, do so in a way that encourages teamwork, rather than aggressive competition. It's about company performance, not individual task.

(3) Market Your Attendance

Use your existing marketing databases to let the existing and potential customers know that you are attending the event. Contact local and trade press to make your appearance known. Is there anything you can use to add more attraction, such as a new product launch?

(4) Stock up and Organize

Do you have enough stock? Get ready with hand-outs, refreshments, and any other items you may need, including spares and batteries. What's the worst that can happen? Plan for it.

2．Perform at the Exhibition

(1) Get the Most from Your Staff

First, make sure your staff are approachable. If your team gets together, discussing a recent visitor to your stand, your stand won't exactly look inviting. Also, get to know which member in your team works best with which kind of visitor. If you make contact with a prospect and your discussions aren't going well, don't be afraid to bring in a more relevant colleague.

Keep the initial positive feeling as the day wears on. You may get tired, but you need to ensure there is support for the whole team. A highly motivated, well-informed team differentiates you from other exhibitors. Regular briefings and teamwork are a must.

(2) Attract and Engage

How can you motivate people to visit your stand? A competition or prize can achieve this. But does it fit in with your brand values and target market? Is there a better way?

Your appropriate marketing messages should filter out casual visitors and draw relevant people in. An outgoing member of your team is encouraged to approach people all over the exhibition. Don't be scared to reject visitors if they are not relevant. Politely filter out wrong-fit visitors. You should have demonstrations and marketing material that answer the questions of your prospects. If you end up with an interested prospect, close in on them gently, taking appropriate contact details. Ensure you take good notes that you will remember when you get back to the office. Remember a few off-topic details so your follow-up is more personal.

(3) Keep It All Business

A friendly environment on your exhibition stand may encourage people to drop in and stay chatting. Do you really want that? Current customers might expect your undivided attention if they appear, but unless they're your main reason for attending the show, try to set aside specific time for them. Communicating with existing contacts is part of the job of an exhibition, but you need to keep it under control.

3．Assessing after the Exhibition

(1) Analyze Success and Failure

When you get back to the office, sit down with the stand staff, and do an assessment of what worked and what didn't. Discuss suggestions for improving performance at future exhibitions.

(2) Measure Your Results

Now is the time to measure your success against the specific, measurable goals you set for yourself before the event. Examine the event in terms of effectiveness to help plan future events and determine future development of your techniques.

Successful sales teams track contacts made at the exhibition up to a year. Only then can you determine the value of the exhibition for your company and whether your marketing budget is well spent.

(3) Follow up All Contacts

Every visitor to your exhibition stand should receive a timely follow-up, such as a simple thank-you letter, phone call or information pack e-mail. You are to remind the prospects your company has products that interest them in the days and weeks following the exhibition.

1. Make the best choice according to the passage.

(1) Exhibitions are welcomed mostly for the following reasons except ____.

A. to interact with audience face-to-face

B. to display newly developed products

C. to sell products on the spot

D. to talk only with existing customers

(2) When one exhibitor is planning and preparing, he has to think about ____.

A. specific goals

B. which staff members should appear

C. how to make others know about his attendance

D. all the above

(3) When stocking up, one exhibitor is getting everything ready except _____.

A. hand-outs   B. refreshments

C. spares   D. nothing special

(4) Exhibiting staff are taught to _____.

A. be approachable

B. be competitive among team members

C. stay huddled (挤在一团)

D. gather around any person if he/she appears at the booth

(5) _____ and teamwork can help keep the positive spirits（高昂的情绪） even when the staff are tired.

A. Criticism   B. Bonus

C. Regular briefings   D. Feedback of the audience

(6) When somebody approaches the booth, what is the best way to react? ____

A. Hand-out a brochure of your products to this visitor.

B. Politely reject this visitor if he/she is a wrong-fit visitor.

C. Inform this visitor of your products with high spirits.

D. Communicate with this visitor warmly if he is an existing customer and ignore passers-by.

(7) Post-exhibition activities are not to be forgotten. The exhibitor needs to _____.

A. have a summary/de-briefing meeting

B. immediately measure the financial results after he gets back to the company

C. follow up only the important contacts

D. find out which visitors are not interested in the products

(8) What is the best time to assess the results of the exhibition?

A. In a month.　　　　B. The time one gets back to the company.

C. Never.　　　　　　D. Up to a year.

2. Translate the following sentences using as many language skills learned in this lesson as possible.

(1) 展品在展会上的曝光率能促进总的销售量。

(2) 展会发放品能有助于观众认识新产品，并使其转化为潜在客户。

(3) 参展商的参展策略包括准备阶段、展中表现、展后总结三个步骤。

(4) 在展会中，当热情逐渐耗尽时，不断地总结归纳和鼓励团队合作能重振士气。

(5) 要礼貌地筛选并推辞掉不合目标的观众，把机会更多地留给对自己的产品感兴趣的目标群体。

Section Ⅳ　The Internet Research

1．What are exhibitors usually concerned with before signing up for an exhibition?

2．When decorating an exhibition booth, what factors does an exhibitor need to consider in general?

3．What are the strategies often used to market the exhibitors' attendance to those existing and potential customers?

Section Ⅴ　New Words You've Met in This Lesson

tactical	adj.	战略的，战术的
interact	vi.	相互作用(影响)，互相配合
specific	adj.	具体的，明确的
acquaint	vt.	使熟悉，使了解
potential	adj.	潜在的，有可能的
target	vt.	瞄准某物
aggressive	adj.	好争斗的，挑衅的，侵略性的
launch	n.	发布
stock	n./v.	存货；储备，保持……的供应
refreshments	n.	提神物；饮料，点心
colleague	n.	同事，同僚
briefing	n.	简要指示，情况简介
filter	vi.	过滤，用过滤法除去
assess	v.	评估
track	v.	跟踪，追踪

Section VI Writing Related to EC Industry

If you are going to attend a show, how would you inform your potential and existing customers that you are going there, and that if they happen to attend it they can come to visit your booth there? List out your choices and tell why with at least 100 words.

Section VII Review of This Unit

1. Jargons in This Unit

product introduction	产品推介
exhibition strategy and style	参展策略和风格
follow-up	后续/后期跟进
existing and potential customers	现有和潜在的客户
overall sales	总销售量/额
awareness of new product	认识新产品
exhibits exposure	展品曝光率/展品宣传
luxury goods	奢侈品
overall visitor promotion and attraction	整体的观众吸引
direct mail	直邮
outbound and inbound exhibitions	出境和入境的展览
first-tier city	一线城市
branding	打出会展场所的知名度
publication of the participation	通知/告知别人将参展

2. Sentence Patterns/Practical Dialogues

(1) To one's disappointment, one didn't find…

(2) The prices of the exhibits vary so much that…

(3) The organizer failed to return the 20% deposit to 50 exhibitors to compensate their losses.

(4) A lot of factors need to be considered before…

(5) As for the location, I highly recommend …

(6) Our tactical and strategic recommendation is to improve…

3. Writing Related to EC Industry

Write alternatives to publicize the participation.

Unit 8

Preparations for the MICE Profession

会展行业入职准备

单元目标

1. 了解会展行业多种从业资格考试。
2. 了解主要国家会展行业的发展前景、趋势及人才要求。
3. 学会看懂会展行业招聘广告,并能够根据要求撰写求职信。
4. 能够应用所学的背景材料和专业术语,使用英文顺畅表达对该行业的看法。

Lesson 1

Career Prospect of MICE
会展行业职业前景

Section I A Sample Dialogue

[Scene] Xu Lei, a senior student from the English Department, is a student reporter for the college newspaper. He is interviewing Mr. Smith, Human Resources manager of Guangdong Yangcheng International Exhibition Company about the career prospects of the MICE industry.

英语专业大四学生徐磊是大学校报的学生记者。他正在采访广州羊城国际会展公司的人力资源经理史密斯先生，了解会展行业的发展前景。

Xu Lei: Good afternoon, Mr. Smith! Thank you for agreeing to this interview.

Smith: Good afternoon, Xu! What do you want to know about MICE?

Xu Lei: We university students are not so familiar with MICE. What does it stand for?

Smith: MICE is an acronym for "Meetings, Incentive Travel, Conventions & Exhibitions".

Xu Lei: Oh, I see. Is MICE a promising industry?

Smith: Indeed. It is a thriving industry. MICE activities play a significant role in strengthening Guangzhou's position as a tourism centre in China and Asia as a whole. Currently, more than 800 MICE events are held in Guangzhou annually. Event organizers such as Yangcheng International have increased their capacity in recent years. Now Guangzhou has more than 6 major International Convention and Exhibition Centers, but before long two new big centers will be ready for use.

Xu Lei: It seems that Guangzhou has been developing at a fast pace in the MICE industry in recent years. What's about the development of the MICE industry in China and Asia?

Smith: Let me answer this question by quoting reliable figures from a UFI's report. UFI (Union of international Fairs), the global association of the exhibition industry, reported last week that the MICE industry in Asia expanded strongly in 2011. Net area sold by organizers in Asia grew by nearly 18% reaching a total of 13.2 million square meters. The fourth edition of UFI's annual report on the MICE market in Asia showed that China remains by far the largest MICE market.

Xu Lei: Wonderful! I'd like to ask you if university students have job opportunities in the exhibition sector. You know we are concerned about job-hunting and future career development.

Unit 8　Preparations for the MICE Profession 会展行业入职准备

Smith: I totally understand. MICE offers a rewarding but demanding career. It also offers opportunities to work with professionals from different backgrounds and cultures. This industry is willing to provide many good job opportunities for new graduates.

Xu Lei: What kind of people do you want to recruit?

Smith: We are looking for people who are energetic and passionate. A bachelor degree is necessary. What's more, proficiency in English is essential as many exhibitors and exposition visitors come from English speaking countries. Qualifications in the MICE industry are needed.

Xu Lei: What kind of employees have better chances of promotion in the MICE industry?

Smith: Best performers in this industry should be able to conceptualize events, exhibitions, conventions and other such meetings. They know how to pitch, present and market the events. Furthermore, they know how to develop creative concepts and transform ideas into stunning layouts and visuals.

Xu Lei: I hope one day I can become a top performer in this industry. Is that possible?

Smith: Of course! Your English is good, which is a precondition for you to work in this industry. If you put effort into your work, you will be successful.

Xu Lei: Thanks for your encouragement. I hope to see you again.

Smith: See you!

1. Read the conversation again and decide whether the following statements are true (T) or false (F).

(1) Mr. Smith is the manager of the Human Resources Department of his company.　(　)

(2) In the near future Guangzhou will have 8 major International Convention and Exhibition Centers.　(　)

(3) The earnings of Mr. Smith's company enjoyed an 18% increase in 2011 compared with the previous year.　(　)

(4) According to UFI's annual report, China was the largest market for MICE in 2011.　(　)

(5) A bachelor degree is the minimum requirement of a job in the MICE industry.　(　)

(6) Proficiency in English is not important for a job in the MICE industry.　(　)

(7) Creativity can enable one working in this industry to get further promotion.　(　)

2. Find reliable materials on the Internet and talk with your partner about the recent development in the MICE industry in your home town. You may compare it with that of Guangzhou shown in the dialogue. Try to point out positive or negative factors affecting the development of the MICE industry in your hometown.

3. Match the jargons on the left with the Chinese equivalents on the right.

(1) recruit　　　　　　　　　a. 人力资源
(2) remuneration　　　　　　b. 净面积
(3) net area　　　　　　　　c. 会议设施
(4) pitch　　　　　　　　　　d. 英语流利

(5) visual
(6) proficiency in English
(7) video conferencing
(8) conference producer
(9) human resources
(10) convention facilities

e. 薪酬
f. 视频会议
g. 视觉资料
h. 招募，招收
i. 推销
j. 会议制作人

Section Ⅱ Communication Activities

1. Pair Work

Please read through the advertisement of "Career Opportunities" posted by a company called MICE Global. Take turns in asking each other simple questions about the requirements of the positions provided by this company.

[Sample dialogue]

A: Do you have a strong aptitude for sales if you want to be a…?

B: Yes (No).

A: Are you self-disciplined?

B: Certainly yes.

Career Opportunities

Want to be a part of a growing company?

Are you self-driven and possess a strong desire to excel?

At MICE Global, we welcome individuals who are positive, motivated, creative, responsible and most importantly have a never-ending desire to learn!

If you have the passion to help our business succeed, send your resume to us at hr@miceglobal.com.sg now!

Available Positions

Corporate Sales Executive

Do you possess a strong aptitude for sales? Are you self-disciplined? Do you enjoy communicating to individuals over the telephone? If you have the above traits, we want you!

As a Corporate Sales Executive, you will be at the forefront to make the events happen! You will be involved in market research, leads generation and communicating to executives worldwide.

Conference Producer

Are you capable of conducting Market Research on cutting edge topics? Can you talk to individuals and find out their challenges? Are you able to negotiate with expert trainers and speakers?

In this position, you should possess excellent communication skills and will have to work closely with internal departments from Sales, Marketing and Operations. You will also be accountable for the events profit and loss.

2. Role Play

Please work in pair and make a dialogue.

[Situation]

A job interview at MICE Global.

Jack: The interviewee

Mr. Thomas: The HR(Human Resource) Manager

[Sample dialogue]

Mr. Thomas: Hello, Jack! Please take a seat. Thank you for choosing our company as your prospective employer.

Jack: I felt so happy when I received a call from the HR department, telling me I could come to have this interview. I'm glad to meet you, Mr. Thomas!

Mr. Thomas: Happy to meet you, too. Now I am going to ask you several questions about your resume. Are you a graduate from…University?

Jack: Yes.

Mr. Thomas: Why do you want to find a job in the MICE industry as you are actually an English major?

Jack: …

[Useful expressions]

Interviewee	The HR Manager
I am looking for a job which can provide me with opportunities and challenges.	This is a growing and promising company.
I am proficient in French, English, and Japanese.	Fluency in foreign languages is wonderful. Also a bachelor degree is necessary, and it is beneficial if you have experience in this industry.
What's special about the job in your company?	You should be prepared to travel around the country and abroad.
May I ask about the remuneration package(薪酬方案)?	The remuneration package is generous and includes travel benefits.
What are other requirements for this job?	You should be passionate and self-motivated, willing to take challenges. You should be able to do market research.

Section Ⅲ Expansion Reading

[导读]

本文摘选自在伦敦工商协会(London Chamber of Commerce and Industry)的资助之下完成的调查报告。该文对全球会议和旅游目的地转移改变，以及未来的前景进行了仔细分析。为了解全球，特别是英国会展行业的就业前景提供了详细资料。

Competitive Forces and Future Prospects of MICE

Specific Destinations

In relation to specific destinations, competition comes from most of the world's continents. The European Union countries, Eastern Europe, the Middle East, Asia, the USA and Australia are all considered as good destinations now. Each of these regions has a competitive advantage.

Competition from the EU is due to the relative lower cost of many of its countries due to the strength of Sterling. Eastern Europe is again seen as low cost and has the advantage of being a new destination that can offer a new type of travel experience. The Middle East has promoted itself as a new and exotic destination. It offers high quality services and accommodation.

The Asian conference products are good value for money as long haul destinations, with a reputation for excellent service and many new state-of-the-art conference venues. North America is benefiting from low cost airfares from Europe, and has a reputation for quality venues and service. Australia has enjoyed a high profile in recent years because of the Sydney 2000 Olympics and is again seen as offering a high quality product.

Specific Technologies

Competition for the UK conference market arises from developments in technology. Key technological areas that act as a competitive force are:

(1) Increased use of the Internet for information means that trade exhibitions are not as busy as in previous usual as clients can research and communicate through the web. Buyers are using websites for research rather than attending exhibitions.

(2) Video conferencing and business communications reduces the need for face-to-face meetings.

(3) An increased willingness from delegates to utilize and expect state-of-the-art technology.

(4) Broadband Internet access - British Telecom's monopoly of telecommunications is hampering the UK's progress. This is due to slow adaptation of broadband facilities that determine access, and high cost.

Other Competitive Forces

In addition to destinations and technologies that are seen as competitive forces for the UK, there are a range of other issues that are areas for potential competition. These can be summarized as:

- Economic;
- Human Resources;
- Infrastructure;
- Marketing;
- Inadequate and/or Incompatible Statistics.

In terms of economic issues the value of sterling in relation to other destinations is seen as a threat. With regard to human resource issues, there is a perceived lack of training of staff, and poor organization of some conferences as a result of poor service quality.

Turning to infrastructure, the UK stock offers little flexibility of venue space compared to other destinations. The marketing of conference destinations and venues is also seen as a potential area for increased competition. The competitiveness of UK destinations is seen as being further constrained by the lack of reliable statistics for the industry.

Future Prospects

The future of the UK conference and meetings industry is clearly dependent on a range of external influences.

In order to remain competitive, the UK conference and meetings industry needs to respond to a number of challenges that will face the industry in the near future. Their response should be:

(1) To upgrade conference venue infrastructure and to develop new products.

(2) To invest in human resource development for the industry in order to become an attractive career option, and to improve employee motivation.

(3) To implement and utilize new technologies that facilitate the successful organization and delivery of conferences and meetings.

(4) To continue to invest in marketing strategies that will raise the profile of the UK conference and meetings industry overseas.

(5) To lobby government for support in terms of funding and investments.

1. Answer the following questions orally according to the passage.

(1) Who are considered powerful competitors for the UK in the conference and meeting marketplace?

(2) What are the reasons for Eastern Europe to be a possible destination that can win trade from the UK in the next five years?

(3) What are Australia's advantages in the tourism market?

(4) In what way did the British broadband access hinder the progress of the British conference industry?

(5) What is the current situation concerning the human resources issue in Britain?

(6) What are the factors influencing the British Conference Market?

(7) What effective measures should be taken by the UK in order to remain competitive in the conference marketplace?

(8) After reading the passage, what suggestions can you give to the Chinese conference market?

2. Translate the following sentences using as many language skills learned in this lesson as possible.

(1) 亚洲会展市场提供的产品很有价值，这是因为亚洲会展成本偏低，有许多高雅先进的会展场馆可供选择。

(2) 2000年悉尼奥运会后，澳大利亚成为世界关注的焦点，它也被认为是一个非常有竞争力的会展市场。

(3) 一系列先进的通信技术的出现，如视频会议，让面对面的会议变得不再如此必要了。

(4) 其他会展目的地国给予其会展行业大量资金支持，这给英国的会展行业带来极大的压力。

(5) 在竞争日益激烈的世界会展市场下，英国的会展行业为了生存不得不去适应各种变化。

(6) 为了促进会展业的进一步发展，伦敦工商会应该游说政府提供资金和投资。

Section Ⅳ The Internet Research

1. Search for more information about future prospects for the MICE industry in China or other countries.

2. Find negative and positive factors affecting the development of the MICE industry in China.

3. Surf on the net for possible posts for graduates in exhibition companies.

Section Ⅴ New Words You've Met in This Lesson

accountable	adj.	负有责任的
aptitude	n.	才能，天资
compound	v.	使严重，恶化
flexibility	n.	弹性，灵活性
demanding	adj.	要求高的
hamper	v.	阻碍
infrastructure	n.	基础设施
incompatible	adj.	不相容的，矛盾的
proficiency	n.	精通，熟练
proximity	n.	近似
promising	adj.	有前景的

Lesson 2

Qualifications for the MICE Profession
会展行业职业资格

Section Ⅰ A Sample Dialogue

[scene] Charles Chan, director of MICE Global, a group of companies involved in MICE, came to speak at the Guangzhou Spring Job Fair at Baiyun International Convention and Exhibition Center. After the speech, Xu Lei, a college student, consulted Mr. Chan about the qualifications for a MICE career.

Unit 8 Preparations for the MICE Profession 会展行业入职准备

查尔斯·陈是全球会展集团的主任,前往广州白云国际会展中心参加广州春季招聘会并对求职者作讲座。会后,大学生徐磊向陈先生咨询了关于会展工作资格的一系列问题。

Xu Lei: Hello, Mr. Chan! I'm Xu Lei from Guangdong University of Foreign Studies.

Charles: Hello, Xu! Nice to meet you!

Xu Lei: Nice to meet you too. Your talk really inspired me a lot. Now I'm thinking about hunting for a job in MICE industry. Would you give me some useful suggestions?

Charles: My pleasure!

Xu Lei: I'm quite interested in convention and exhibition organization. I just want to know more about the requirements for a job in this industry.

Charles: I am so glad that you have decided on a career as a PCO(Professional Conference Organizer) or PEO (Professional Exhibition Organizer), which will be very rewarding in the future. As for requirements, we are looking for people who have skill, experience and aptitude in conceptualizing, planning, managing and promoting an event. If you can prove your have potential, you are badly needed.

Xu Lei: Oh, I see. Is it necessary for job seekers to have a specialized degree to join the MICE industry?

Charles: A specialized degree is not always needed. But of course, a relevant degree would be useful to provide you with a solid foundation, especially in marketing, tourism, business and related fields. For instance, a graduate with a bachelor degree in Commerce with double majors in Hospitality & Tourism Management and Marketing Management will be much welcomed.

Xu Lei: It's a pity I don't have a specialized degree. I major in English.

Charles: We welcome graduates with a bachelor degree in English. Language competence is quite important in this industry as the staff have to communicate with professionals from different backgrounds and cultures. Interpersonal relationships can be easily established without language barriers. Your major will be an advantage for you when you plunge into this industry.

Xu Lei: What should I do to develop my professional skills?

Charles: You may work as an intern in an exhibition company and learn from experience. Meanwhile, you can study hard to get some qualifications in the MICE industry.

Xu Lei: What are the qualifications?

Charles: In China, there are accreditations for Convention and Exhibition Interpreters, Convention and Exhibition Strategists, Convention and Exhibition Designers, Convention and Exhibition Managers, Convention and Exhibition Organizers, etc. You may challenge yourself by taking the qualification examination of Convention and Exhibition Interpreters.

Xu Lei: I'm quite interested in this. Do you think it can offer me good opportunities for career development?

Charles: I'm sure if you work hard, you will find the work very rewarding.

Xu Lei: I hope one day I can realize my dream of being a professional working in a transnational MICE company.

Charles: Being visionary is a good thing for young men. After several years in the MICE industry, you may find chances to get the globally recognized MICE industry training, leading towards the attainment of the Certified Meeting Professional (CMP) global certification. This certificate will enable you to work everywhere in the world in this industry.

Xu Lei: That will surely be what I am striving for.

Charles: Good luck to you!

Xu Lei: Thanks for your encouragement and suggestions.

Charles: You're welcome!

1. Please answer the following questions according to the passage.

(1) What did Charles Chan do at the Guangzhou Spring Job Fair?

(2) What employees are badly needed by exhibition companies according to Mr. Chan?

(3) What was the major of Xu Lei? Where did he study?

(4) What was the reason for Xu's major being an advantage in this industry?

(5) What steps would Xu take to become a professional in the MICE industry?

(6) What are the qualification exams mentioned in the dialogue?

(7) What is CMP according to the dialogue?

(8) What is the benefit of having a CMP?

2. Discuss in groups and work out the brainstorm map.

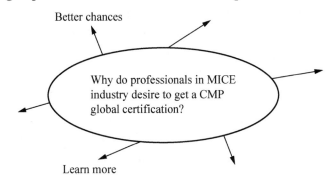

3. Match the jargons on the left with the Chinese equivalents on the right.

(1) visionary   a. 人际关系
(2) PCO   b. 策划师
(3) MPI   c. 有远见的
(4) interpersonal relationship   d. 合格证明
(5) intern   e. 营销
(6) accreditation   f. 职业会议组织者

Unit 8 Preparations for the MICE Profession 会展行业入职准备

(7) qualification   g. 资格
(8) ROI   h. 实习
(9) strategist   i. 投资回报率
(10) marketing   j. 国际会议专家联盟

Section II Communication Activities

1. Pair Work

Please study the contents of the chart below. Take turns to ask each other about the qualification examinations that interest you.

Variety	Precondition	Subjects	Benefits	Problems
C&E Interpreter (C& E is the short form for Convention and Exhibition)	College education with English certificate such as CET-4	Written Exam; Oral Interpretation	Suitable for English majors. Urgently needed by this industry	Exam for elementary interpreters; Not as competitive as CATTI certificate holders
C&E Planner	2-year college education possibly with experience in C&E planning	Basic Theories of C&E; Official Documents and Letters of C&E; Practical English in MICE (written and oral); C&E Expertise (C&E management or C&E Marketing)	Urgently needed by this industry; Low requirements for exam takers	English majors should learn additional courses to pass the exam; Time-consuming and demanding
C&E Strategist	College graduates in related majors	C&E Program Investigation; C&E Program Planning; C&E Program Marketing; C&E Program Management	Urgently needed by this industry; Better paid; Good future prospects in this industry	English majors should learn additional courses to pass the exam; Time-consuming and effort-taking
International Commercial C&E Organizer	College graduates in related majors	Fundamentals in International Commercial C&E; International Commercial C&E Management and Marketing	Urgently needed by this industry; Better opportunities to work with people from different backgrounds and cultures	English majors should learn additional courses to pass the exam; Time-consuming and demanding

2. Role Play

Please finish the dialogue with your partner by using the information listed in the chart above. Remember to exchange roles and make a new dialogue.

[Situation] In consultation with an expert in Student Career Guidance Center

Student A: One who is graduating from the college
Mr. Davis: The expert
[Sample dialogue]
Student A: Good morning, Mr. Davis! I'm hoping you have some time to give me valuable advice.
Mr. Davis: My pleasure, young lady/man. Please be seated and tell me what you want to know.
Student A: I'm graduating in 4 months and I'm considering taking a job in the MICE industry. I understand entry into this industry demands qualifications. I am really confused which qualification exam I should take. You know, currently there are more than 10 qualification exams for this industry.
Mr. Davis: Oh, I see. What are the qualification exams you know about?
Student A: There are …
Mr. Davis: First tell me which exam you are most interested in.
Student A: I'm interested in …
Mr. Davis: Firstly, we should go over the preconditions for the exams. You have to find out if you are eligible for the exams. Secondly, we have to evaluate the benefits and disadvantages of taking these exams.
Student A: That's what I am here for. Let me show you all the information about the exams and then could you please give me some suggestions?
Mr. Davis: Okay!
…

Section III Expansion Reading

[导读]

本文介绍了会展行业中相关的人力资源类问题，阐述了该行业的技术要求和发展机会，并介绍了此行业的发展趋势，还大篇幅介绍了各国各地的会展专业教育及相关培训信息。

Human Resource Issues for the Convention Industry

Introduction

The size, scope and labor intensity of the global meetings and convention industry decide the paramount importance of effective human resource policies and practices. Until recently, it was mainly professional associations such as ICCA(International Congress & Convention Association), and IAPCO(The International Association of Professional Congress Organizers) that offered education programs relevant to the industry. In the past decade, however, significant efforts have been made to correct this situation. In view of increased globalization, attempts are also being made to create links in education programs worldwide.

Employment Opportunities and Skill Requirements

Traditionally no vocational training has been available in the MICE industry, and management positions are generally taken up by people from related industries. Furthermore, education and training programs offered by both national and international industry associations, and more recently by universities, have generally been of a sporadic nature.

The MICE sector offers a wide range of employment opportunities, primarily with organizers of meetings and conventions, venue operators (e.g., convention centers, convention hotels), supporting service providers (e.g., technical support firms), and independent PCOs (Professional Conference Organizer). As the convention industry is essentially a service industry, with people taking a central role, it follows that interpersonal skills are critical for those working in the MICE sector. Organizational, negotiation and communication skills, creativity, flexibility, and a team player mentality are further important requirements, in addition to job specific competencies.

Adult Education

There is a growing realization that members of the MICE industry are more involved in the field of adult education than many had previously realized. Convention attendees have access to alternative forms of media that compete with the convention to provide them with educational and networking services. Managers in the meeting and convention industry will increasingly need to understand the fundamentals of adult education and learning to ensure an effective ROI(Return On Investment) to their customers.

Education and Training Programs for the Convention Industry

Education at all levels is critical to the growth of the MICE industry. The benefits of education are self-perpetuating. Businesses that are informed of increased performance levels attainable through effective conferences and meetings are more likely to invest in these activities. Education is equally important, if not more so, at a grass root level. The demand for highly skilled employees is driven by the number of new MICE facilities being built throughout the world and increased sophistication of the industry and its customers.

Education Programs in North America—Industry Associations

North America is currently the global hub of MICE industry education and certification programs. PCMA(Professional Convention Management Association) and IACVB (International Association of Convention & Visitor Bureaus) are two of the largest and most powerful industry associations. Both have an educational foundation that is supported by generous financial endowments and operated at arm's length from the associations. They offer a number of industry education and certification programs, either in-house or in cooperation with each other, industry partners, or universities.

Education Programs in North America—Universities

A significant number of institutions that offer programs tailored to the tourism and hospitality disciplines also include at least one MICE industry course within the existing tourism/hospitality curriculum. The University of Nevada, Las Vegas, is a leader in MICE education, not only at the national but also at the international level. Its tourism and convention department offers as a concentration in the bachelor of hotel administration degree area sixteen courses that focus on various aspects of the MICE industry. Courses taught include meeting planning, destination marketing, incentive travel, association management, convention facility management, and trade show operations.

Notes

(1) ICCA(International Congress & Convention Association)：国际大会及会议协会，创建于 1963 年，是全球会议业最主要的国际专业组织之一。其成员涵盖了国际会务活动的操作执行、运输及住宿等各相关领域。

(2) IAPCO(International Association of Professional Congress Organizers)：国际专业会议组织者协会，成立于 1968 年，是一个由专业的国际国内会议、特殊活动组织者及管理者组成的非营利性组织，服务于全球的专业会议组织者。

(3) ROI(Return On Investment)：投资回报率，是指通过投资而应返回的价值，它涵盖了企业的获利目标。

(4) IACVB(International Association of Convention & Visitor Bureaus)：国际会议和观光局联合会，1914 年创立，是目前世界上最大的非营利性质的会议和观光局协会，有来自 30 个国家、大约 500 个目的地管理机构的 1,200 多名成员。IACVB 为其成员提供教育资源和网络机会，并为公众提供会议和观光产业(CVB industry)的信息。网址：http://www.iacvb.org/iacvb/index.asp.

(5) PCMA(Professional Convention Management Association)：专业会议管理协会，1957 年成立于美国费城，是一个非营利性质的国际会展业专业协会，总部设在美国芝加哥。其职业策划/规划成员每年预订的会议超过 30,000 次，其合作供应商(supplier partner)来自航空、旅馆、会议局(convention bureaus)和音像公司，这两类成员及其单位每年创造成果 1,000 亿美元的相关收入。

1. Answer the following questions orally according to the passage.

(1) What are typical of training programs for MICE professionals?
(2) What are the job opportunities offered by the MICE sector?
(3) What are the important requirements in relation to job competencies?
(4) What can be considered key priorities in human resource development?
(5) What are the reasons for the concern about adult education in MICE sector?
(6) Where is the center of the MICE industry education and certification program?
(7) What kinds of programs are offered by the leading industry associations in North America?
(8) What courses are offered by the University of Nevada, a leader in MICE education?

2. Translate the following sentences using as many language skills learned in this lesson as possible.

(1) 全球会展行业的规模、范围及劳动力密集程度，决定了有效的人力资源政策和规定是极其重要的。

(2) 会展行业就业的一大特点是以往从未有这样的职业培训项目，而经理职位通常是由相关行业的人士来担任。

(3) 由于会展行业首先是一种服务行业，在这种行业中，人力占据中心地位，因此人际关系对此行业的从业人员是很重要的。

(4) 被动的会展公司将处于一种危险的境况中，它们将不得不随波逐流，这种做法在竞争日益激烈的今天无疑是导致其破产的商业策略。

(5) 会展行业的经理们愈加需要了解成人教育的基本原则，以确保客户的投资回报率。

(6) 全世界范围内新的会展设施数量越来越多，会展行业与会展客户情况越来越复杂，因此行业需要技术娴熟、知识丰富的雇员。

Section Ⅳ The Internet Research

1. Search for more information about qualification exams in the MICE industry.
2. Try to collect information about reliable education providers in this industry in China.

Section Ⅴ New Words You've Met in This Lesson

accreditation	n.	合格证明
eligible	adj.	符合资格的
endowment	n.	捐赠，基金
hub	n.	中心
in-house	adj.	在机构内部的
intern	n.	实习
sporadic	adj.	零星的，时有时无的
ROI		投资回报率
time-consuming	adj.	花时间的
vocational	adj.	职业的

Section Ⅵ Writing Related to EC Industry

1. Please read the job advertisement.

Business Development Manager Recruitment

Company: Arch International Media Ltd.
Position: Business Development Manager
Type: Full time job
Experience: More than 3 years
Degree Required: Bachelor degree or above
Language: Chinese, English
Location: Beijing
Ideal Candidate

(1) Minimum 3 years' experience of marketing sales at an international brand hotel(5 star), tourism board or convention bureau.

(2) An understanding of how marketing strategies work in the meeting industry; be

specialized in planning and executing marketing of hotel meeting.

(3) Ability to write emails, business proposals and speak well both in Chinese and English.

(4) Having a passion for the meeting, incentive and media industry; be extrovert, appropriately dressed, articulate and healthy.

(5) Bachelor degree or above in hotel, English, tourism, advertising, or marketing sales.

(6) 26 years old or above.

Career Development

(1) MICE China provides you a broad platform to access the global meeting industry.

(2) MICE China brings you the leading positions in the meeting industry.

(3) Be able to access to the whole industry chain, which provide you rich opportunities working in the meeting industry.

(4) Performance-based payment system.

Managing Director: David Zhong
Email: david.zhong@micechina.com
Mobile: 13911139911
Tel: +8610-84466451/2/3 ext.6166
Fax: +8610-84466451/2/3 ext.6110

2. Assume you are qualified for the post. Write to *david.zhong@micechina.com* an application letter.

Section VII Review of This Unit

1. Jargons in This Unit

career prospect	职业前景
tourism center	旅游中心
net area	净面积，实用面积
qualification exam	资质考试
remuneration package	薪酬方案
human resource department	人力资源部，人事部
competitive advantage	竞争优势
long haul destination	长途目的地
state-of-the-art conference venue	最先进/高级的会议场所
a high profile	引人注目的形象
conference venue infrastructure	会议场所基础设施
certified meeting professionals	有证书的会议专业人才
education and training programs	教育和培训项目
supporting service provider	配套商；服务商
job specific competency	具体工作能力；特定业务能力

2. Sentence Patterns/Practical Dialogues

(1) A: Please take a seat. Thank you for choosing our company as your prospective employer.

B: I felt so happy when I received a call from the HR department, telling me I could come to have this interview.

(2) A: Well, we've evaluated a lot of resumes and we are interested in yours.

B: Thank you.

A: Now I am going to ask you several questions about your resume.

B: Go ahead.

(3) A: What's special about the job in your company?

B: You should be prepared to travel in and outside of the country.

(4) A: May I ask about the remuneration package?

B: The remuneration package is generous including travel benefits.

(5) A: What are other requirements for this job?

B: You should be passionate and self-motivated, willing to take challenges. You should be able to do market research.

3. Writing Related to EC Industry

Write an application letter for a position at a convention/ exhibition company.

参考答案

Unit 1　Introduction of MICE Industry at Home and Abroad

Lesson 1　Introduction of the World MICE Industry

Section Ⅰ

1. (1) T　(2) T　(3) T　(4) T　(5) F　(6) F　(7) T　(8) F

2. In groups, discuss what is "会展".

会展业(MICE industry)简称 MICE，包括会议(meeting)、奖励旅游(incentive tour)、研讨会(conference)和展览(exhibition or event)。

狭义的会展业(convention & exhibition industry)包括展览会(fairs)、集市(markets)、展销会(sales)、交易会(consumer and trade shows)、博览会(expositions)和会议(meetings and conventions)。

3. (1) c　(2) i　(3) b　(4) a　(5) f　(6) d　(7) g　(8) j　(9) e　(10) h

Section Ⅲ

1. (1) D　(2) D　(3) B　(4) D　(5) C　(6) C　(7) C　(8) A

2. Translation

(1) Organizing a meeting or incentive trip involves moving around vast amounts of information.

(2) The new trend in organizing meetings is to make them shorter and smaller, but hold them more frequently.

(3) The new trend in incentive travel is to shrink the number of participants per incentive group, hold event in domestic venues or in destinations nearer to the participants home, and to arrange more free time arrangement.

(4) The tough economic situation has brought the MICE industry a choice: whether to hold corporate events in the domestic market or to spend big money overseas.

(5) Although British organizers tend to hold their events in their domestic market, Americans see international expansion as the best route to promoting MICE industry, spending a lot to attract overseas attendees.

Lesson 2　Yesterday and Today of China's MICE Industry

Section Ⅰ

1. Answer the following questions

(1) Due to cultural differences in doing business (for example, government's red tape and

reliance on personal relationships with authorities and associations).

(2) Messe Dusseldorf, Messe Hannover, Messe·Munchen, and China's Shanghai Putong Land Development Corporation.

(3) He implies that although we are using the same terms, we are not actually doing the same industry/business because Chinese exhibitions are unique.

(4) International exhibitions are those exhibitions with foreign exhibitors making up at least 10% of the total number of exhibitors, or with at least 5 % being relevant foreign visitors.

(5) Not necessarily.

(6) Yes, it is. But In the western world, not every show is open to any visitor.

(7) Due to an oversupply of exhibition centers, many less-used exhibition centers are doing this to win chances and customers.

(8) It's destructive in the long run, because it may cause ill competition. The sound order of the industry will be damaged.

2. Discuss in Groups

There exist strong relationships between exhibition organizers, exhibitors, visitors, and exhibition centers; likewise, between exhibitors, decoration contractors and other stakeholders. Outside the main core, there are the government supporting and regulating authorities, public service, middlemen and agents. Public service includes customs, inspection and regulatory authorities, commerce and industry, police and security, fire department, and urban administration.

(1) The major parties of a convention or an exhibition event are organizers, exhibitors, visitors, and contractors.

(2) The relationship among these parties is as follows: to the organizer, there are two kinds of customers —exhibitors and visitors, and they are equally important. A successful player in the industry needs to listen to the needs of both groups. Exhibitors are there to attract visitors and encourage them to buy the products at the exhibition or afterwards.

3. (1) c (2) i (3) b (4) a (5) d (6) e (7) f (8) j (9) g (10) h

Section Ⅲ

1. (1) T (2) F (3) F (4) T (5) T (6) T (7) T (8) T

2. Translation

(1) The exhibition industry (MICE industry) involves a variety of parties, which chiefly include organizers, exhibitors, contractors, visitors, and sponsors.

(2) Exhibitions can be classified differently. For instance they can be classified as specialized exhibitions, consumer exhibitions, and general exhibitions.

(3) Depending on the intervals, exhibitions can be classified into regular and non-regular exhibitions.

(4) According to the sources of exhibitors, exhibitions are divided into local, national and international exhibitions.

(5) The exhibition is a channel which provides face-to-face contacts and business information to traders and suppliers.

Unit 2 Exhibition and Conference Centers in China

Lesson 1 Size and Location of Exhibition Centers

Section I

1. (1) T (2) F (3) F (4) F (5) F (6) T (7) T (8) T

3. (1) c (2) b (3) a (4) d (5) f (6) h (7) j (8) i (9) g (10) e

Section III

1. (1) C (2) D (3) C (4) C (5) C (6) C (7) B (8) B

2. Translation

(1) In terms of spatial distribution, the quantity of exhibitions in the eastern part of China is far larger than that in the western and central areas.

(2) Exhibitions concentrate on 5 regions in China. They are Pearl River Delta, Yangtze River Delta, Bohai Rim, Central China and Western China.

(3) China World Trade Center, located in Beijing, is the market leader in the industry and is widely known as "The Place Where China Meets the World".

(4) Most exhibition centers are equipped with wireless and broadband Internet access, and LCD TVs.

(5) Shanghai New International Expo Center is a joint-venture of Shanghai Pudong Land Development Company and 3 world-famous exhibition centers from Germany.

Lesson 2 Space Size and Location

Section I

1. (1) T (2) T (3) T (4) F (5) F (6) F (7) T (8) T

2. Discuss in groups

Press conference/seminar fee includes meeting room rental, desks, chairs, screen, microphone, AV equipment, water and promotion on show directory.

3. (1) f (2) I (3) j (4) g (5) d (6) h (7) a (8) c (9) b (10) e

Section III

1. Ture or False

(1) False   ref: Standard booth is much more expensive.

(2) True

(3) True   ref: $1,500 per booth × 7= 10,500   10,500−7,800 = ¥2,700

(4) True

(5) True

(6) False   ref: The rent rate varies according to the minimum area, e.g. $36m^2$ ¥780 per m^2; $54 m^2$ ¥680 per m^2.

(7) True

(8) True

2. Translation

A: Hello! I'd like to sign up for the City Gardening Expo. Can I sign up on the phone?

B: Of course, you can. But we won't assign you the booth number until we receive your registration fees.

A: OK. Please reserve a standard booth for me.

B: Which do you prefer, a stand on the ground floor or on the second floor?

A: Do the prices depend on the location?

B. Yes. The ground floor is a better choice so it is more expensive. But if you choose a stand on the second floor, you'll get an extra space of 2 square meters free of charge.

A: Then a stand on the second floor.

B: No problem. The rent rate for a standard booth on the second floor is 12,000 RMB.

Unit 3   Preparations for the Exhibition

Lesson 1   Preparations by the Host

Section I

1. (1) F   (2) T   (3) T   (4) F   (5) F   (6) T   (7) F   (8) T

2. open

3. (1) f   (2) e   (3) b   (4) g   (5) c   (6) d   (7) a   (8) i   (9) j   (10) h

Section III

1. Answer the following questions

(1) Its full name is the 10th China International Trade Show for Exhibition and Conference Industry.

(2) InterExpo 2009 is held in Nanjing International Exhibition Center.

(3) The China Council for the Promotion of International Trade (CCPIT), the Global Association of the Exhibition Industry (UFI), the International Association of Exhibitions and Events (IAEE) and the Society of Independent Show Organizers(SISO) are the sponsors.

(4) China Association for Exhibition Centers and China International Exhibition Center Group Corporation are the organizers.

(5) The theme of the InterExpo 2009 is "Dialogue · Communication · Harmony · Development".

(6) The objective of InterExpo 2009 is to facilitate the development of China's exhibition industry and promote exchange and fair competition within the industry.

(7) The convention lasts for 3 days from January 14th~16th, 2009.

(8) InterExpo 2009 exhibits organizers, fairground owners, booth contractors, service

suppliers, government bodies, exhibition media, etc.

2. Translation

(1) Sponsors　　(2) Organizer　　(3) Co-organizers

(4) You can not only find the theme and objective of this exhibition, but also reserve booths online.

(5) This fair will exhibit the most up-date IT products in the world and hold a symposium on the development of IT industry.

(6) The theme of this exposition is finalized to be: City, Development and Harmony.

(7) The move-in and move-out dates are decided and sent through text messages to all the exhibitors.

Lesson 2　Preparations by the Exhibitors

Section Ⅰ

1. Answer the following questions

(1) Betty knows about World Expo from the news in China Daily at the beginning.

(2) World Expo shows human inspirations and thoughts.

(3) Expo 2010 Shanghai China will be the first World Exposition in a developing country.

(4) Because fifty-five percent of the world population is expected to live in cities by the year 2010.

(5) About 200 countries or cities will participate in this exposition.

(6) The name of the mascot of World Expo 2010 is "Haibao". This is created from a Chinese character meaning people embodying the character of Chinese culture.

(7) The emblem symbolizes the big family of mankind.

(8) World Expo 2010 will be held from May 1 to October 31, 2010.

3. (1) e　(2) c　(3) a　(4) j　(5) i　(6) d　(7) b　(8) f　(9) h　(10) g

Section Ⅲ

1. (1) F　(2) T　(3) T　(4) T　(5) T　(6) F　(7) T　(8) T

2. Translation

(1) Exhibitor lists, visitor numbers and research from the previous year's shows can demonstrate the level of an exhibition.

(2) This is the largest clothing fair in the world held in New York from September 8 to September 11 every year.

(3) Chinese Export Commodities Fair is featured by traditional Chinese culture and modernization.

(4) A successful fair can not only attract businessmen from home and abroad, but also make a fortune from it.

(5) Technical staff can answer questions which the sales people can not.

Unit 4 Participation in an Exhibition

Lesson 1 Decorating: Stand Construction and Reception

Section Ⅰ

1. (1) F (2) F (3) T (4) T (5) F (6) T (7) F (8) F
3. (1) f (2) h (3) g (4) a (5) c (6) e (7) d (8) j (9) b (10) i

Section Ⅲ

1. Answer the following questions

(1) Pico IES Group Ltd.

(2) The official show contractor is responsible for all shell scheme package booths.

(3) The exhibitor's contractor can construct booth interiors and any freestanding displays or fittings that may be required. These are subject to the rules and regulations set by the organizer. It can't do any decorations violating the rules and regulations.

(4) Flashing lights can be put up when they form an integral part of the Exhibitor's products.

(5) A badge issued by the official show contractor.

(6) The exhibitor.

(7) Open frontages mean that the front of the stand should face an aisle.

(8) The government authorities and the organizer.

2. Translation

(1) During the build-up period, exhibitors and their contractors will be responsible for the daily removal of construction and packaging debris off site.

(2) No stand structure, decoration, exhibit or display or furnishings may extend beyond the boundaries of the stand.

(3) The debris of stand construction must be handled in time; otherwise, the exhibitor will be liable for the service fees involved in removing the debris if this is not complied.

(4) All stands in the exhibition, irrespective of height, must have at least half of any frontage facing an aisle open.

(5) Exhibitors and their stand decorators must submit 3 sets of construction drawings of the stand o the organizer before the deadline.

Lesson 2 Promotion of Exhibits, Services Provided and Delegations

Section Ⅰ

1. (1) F (2) T (3) F (4) T (5) F (6) F (7) T (8) F
3. (1) e (2) h (3) i (4) f (5) a (6) b (7) c (8) j (9) d (10) g

Section Ⅲ

1. Answer the following questions

(1) Right literature and giveaways strategies.

(2) "The 'load' em up" people and "the 'give' em nothing" people.

(3) "The 'load' em up" means giving a lot of useful literature to show visitors; "the 'give' em nothing" means giving no literature to show visitors.

(4) If a complex product is sold and literature only will hinder the purchasing process, the exhibitor can bring no literature but hire a product expert talk to the potential buyer.

(5) If your product is easy to understand, bring the best and most appropriate literature for the show.

(6) A show-specific brochure is a promotional piece that's concise and targeted.

(7) Select items that reflect the quality of your company and can give your business. The kind of giveaways should be something really useful, and it should be kept in a place where potential buyers will refer to it when the need for your products arises.

(8) You can use giveaways to trade for personal information of potential buyers. You can make visitors earn the giveaways, giving their deep impression on your company.

2. Translation

(1) To attract potential buyers, right literature strategy should be adopted.

(2) If the literature provided by the exhibitor doesn't meet the needs of potential buyers, the exhibitor will lose customers.

(3) Use the most appropriate literature for the show and display sample copies.

(4) Giveaways can bring you a lot of customers.

(5) Some exhibitors use giveaways to visitors, purporting to get personal information of customers and learn their likings.

Lesson 3　Emergencies during the Exhibition

Section Ⅰ

1. (1) F　(2) F　(3) T　(4) F　(5) F　(6) F　(7) F　(8) F
3. (1) e　(2) f　(3) h　(4) a　(5) c　(6) b　(7) i　(8) d　(9) j　(10) g

Section Ⅲ

1. Answer the following questions

(1) Natural disasters; facility issues; health issues; potential hazards; labor strikes; political demonstrations; terrorist acts or threats of terrorism, bomb threats; transportation issues; government-mandated closures or travel restrictions, declaration of war.

(2) List names and cell numbers of all key staff, site personnel and contractor, plus your insurance agent's contact information. Radios are essential if cell service goes down. Spell out step-by-step what's to be done and who should be contacted by which staff in various scenarios. List the designated emergency meeting areas for staff both inside and outside the building and in the principal hotel. Include specific wording for messages to audiences if a disruption/ emergency occurs on site. Provide a form to report incidents. Designate where such forms will be available on site. Provide floor diagrams marked with exits and house phones for calling into facility offices.

(3) Show director/manager; exhibit sales team; key on-site staff or vendors (registration, IT

and AV); contractor liaison; building liaison; organization CEO; on-site volunteers/moderators who may be in charge of areas involving large groups (such as a general session); PR staff; call center for exhibitors and/or attendees.

(4) They should undergo trainings.

(5) Take care of people and property first.

(6) People and property should be taken care of first.

(7) The show director CEO or an association board of directors may make the decision.

(8) He who cancels bears the liability.

2. Translation

(1) If there is communications failure during the conference, please contact the organizer as soon as possible.

(2) A complete emergency plan is supposed to include every possibility, such as natural disasters, contagious epidemics and labor strikes.

(3) Names and cell numbers of all convention staff and contractor, plus the insurance agent's contact information should be listed in the disaster plan.

(4) After you've resolved the emergency, hold a roundtable discuss to review lessons and explore a better solution to the disruption.

(5) According to the rule of thumbs for convention and exhibition, any show, large or small, should be insured for its safety.

Unit 5　Cancellation and Move-out

Lesson 1　Cancellation of Exhibit Registration

Section Ⅰ

1. (1) F　(2) F　(3) F　(4) T　(5) F　(6) T　(7) F　(8) T

3. (1) f　(2) h　(3) d　(4) g　(5) c　(6) a　(7) b　(8) e

Section Ⅲ

1. (1) F　(2) F　(3) F　(4) F　(5) F　(6) T　(7) T　(8) F

2. Translation

A: Good morning! I am the sales manager from Shanghai Datong Trade Company. I want to cancel the reservation made six months ago.

B: Oh, it's a pity! The exhibition will open in less than a month.

A: I am really sorry about that. Because of some technical reasons, we can't attend the fair.

B: All right. According to the contract, we will keep 60% of the refund.

A: Oh, can you transfer the rest of the money back to me?

B: Could you please tell me your reserved booth number?

A: Our booth number is E039.

B: OK, we will transfer the rest of the down payment to you.

A: When can I receive the money?

B: According to the regulations, the money will be sent to you after the end of the fair.

Lesson 2　Move-out

Section Ⅰ

1. (1) F　(2) F　(3) T　(4) T　(5) F　(6) F　(7) T　(8) T

2. (1) in advance　　(2) move out　(3) reserved

(4) express appreciation　　　(5) had appointed

3. (1) e　(2) a　(3) c　(4) d　(5) b　(6) h　(7) f　(8) g

Section Ⅲ

1. (1) F　(2) T　(3) T　(4) T　(5) T　(6) F　(7) F　(8) F

2. Translation

(1) People usually ignore post-trade show evaluation and follow-up.

(2) If you have such a habit, you can predict the effects of the next exhibition.

(3) After the exhibition, you should think about what you have learned from others.

(4) When you get back to your office, you should not rush to start a new project.

(5) You should send E-mails to all the visitors who have provided contact information.

Unit 6　Post-Conference Tour

Section Ⅰ

1. (1) F　(2) F　(3) T　(4) F　(5) F　(6) T　(7) T　(8) T

3. (1) d　(2) g　(3) h　(4) f　(5) b　(6) c　(7) i　(8) e　(9) j　(10) a

Section Ⅲ

1. Answer the following questions

(1) Tasmanian World Heritage Area: Cradle Mountain.

(2) The tour aims to highlight the Tasmanian Wilderness World Heritage area, its values and importance—including geology, flora, fauna and conservation—and to gain first-hand experience of the research and conservation programs being undertaken in this area.

(3) It lasts three days and two nights.

(4) The total cost (based on twin share accommodation) is $690.00/person.

Extra cost single room supplements ($190) $880.00/person.

(5) Warm clothing is essential including waterproof coat, woolen hat and gloves, good walking shoes or boots.

(6) Children are not encouraged to take part while partners of science teachers are welcome.

(7) $200 per person.

(8) Through post-conference tours, attendees can better understand the themes of the conferences. Meanwhile, they can also get relaxation after having conferences. (You can also give your suggestions)

2. Translation

(1) It is your free time to go around the place after 3 p.m. on July 8.

(2) This area boasts typical karst features. You'll have a good chance to visit magnificent gorges and intriguing caves.

(3) Please attend a workshop after supper to discuss about the endangered species conservation and Protected Site Management.

(4) Activities will be weather dependent, so be prepared for flexibility in the schedule.

(5) A: Good morning. What can I do for you?

B: Hi. I want to get some information about a one-day city sightseeing. Before I came to this city, I heard it was a city with unique features.

A: This is a city rich in scenic spots. My travel agency can tailor a one-day itinerary to meet your requirements.

B: Great! May I pay a visit to your travel agency and discuss about the itinerary. There are quite a lot of people in my group with different preferences.

A: Sure! I'm confident my agency will tailor travel arrangements to meet individual demands. Considering the scale of your group, I think a package tour will be fine with you.

B: Good. I'll fetch the travel brochure and discuss about the itinerary this afternoon.

A: Okay, see you then.

B: See you.

Unit 7 Exhibition and Conference Strategies

Lesson 1 Organizers' Strategies

Section Ⅰ

1. (1) T (2) T (3) T (4) T (5) F (6) F (7) F (8) T

2. 在中国，展览的主办单位很多是政府主管部门或半官方性质的行业协会，承办单位是一家或几家专业展览公司。这与西方发达国家不同，西方国家展览业已高度市场化，因此大多主办单位和承办单位合二为一，没有所谓的承办单位。而且主办单位大多是专业办展公司，一些工作外包给其他公司做。

此外，在中国，一些专业的展览公司为寻求政府或行业协会的支持，充分利用其对企业的影响力，主动与其合作，邀请政府做或与政府共同做主办单位，但主要的工作由专业的展览公司来做。

3. (1) d (2) g (3) e (4) a (5) j (6) b (7) c (8) f (9) h (10) i

Section Ⅲ

1. Answer the following questions

(1) Exhibitors focus on individual exhibitor performance, while an organizer is concerned with collective exhibitor performance.

(2) Everyone has his own idea. But generally speaking Eos are to (a) satisfy customers, (b)

provide employees with jobs, and (c) make money. (Other suggestions are welcome)

(3) Marketing strategies, direct mailing, using international agents and advisory committees, etc.

(4) Via direct mailing, ads, international agents, etc.

(5) Branding means "打出会展场所的知名度" in Chinese. It provides another competitive advantage. An exhibition must be large in scale and include all the top branded exhibitors in its market, thereby promoting its fame and attraction.

(6) It was efficient, low cost, and measurable.

(7) International agents are recommended to attract overseas exhibitors because their most immediate advantage was an existing command of the language and business customs of the target market.

(8) The function of sponsors is to promote reputation and importance.

2. Translation

(1) The exhibitors who participated in this show have planned to sue the organizer.

(2) The organizer failed to return 15% of the deposits to the exhibitors as it promised.

(3) The exhibition organizer is concerned with collective exhibitor performance, while the individual exhibitors focus more on the location and size of their booths.

(4) The organizer can make use of many marketing strategies to attract exhibitors, such as branding the exhibition venues, advertising, and even hiring international agents.

(5) The role of sponsors can not be neglected for they attract high-quality attendees.

Lesson 2　Exhibitors' Strategies

Section Ⅰ

1. Answer the following questions

(1) They are going to participate in an international tools exhibition. But they are uncertain of the strategy and style.

(2) The strategy and style of their exhibition.

(3) Exhibition strategy and style cannot be considered separately. Although they differ, they share a lot in common. They determine each other.

(4) The aims are to sell goods, expose the exhibits, sign booth contacts, promote overall sales, and raise visitors' awareness of new products.

(5) First, Plan and prepare well. Second, perform well at the exhibition. And finally, assess effectively and follow up closely after the exhibition.

(6) Yes, he partly agrees with the 3 steps. But he proposes detailed arrangement under each step.

(7) To write a plan of their strategy and style in 3 days.

(8) Not totally satisfying. Because the manager says at the beginning at the meeting that "By the end of the meeting, we need to determine the strategy and style of our exhibition", but

determination is to be made in another 3 days.

3. (1) d　(2) c　(3) b　(4) f　(5) a　(6) g　(7) i　(8) e　(9) j　(10) h

Section III

1. (1) D　(2) D　(3) D　(4) A　(5) C　(6) B (A & C are not appropriate if the visitor does not fit in/ is a casual passer-by)　(7) A　(8) D

2. Translation

(1) Exhibit exposure helps enhance the overall sales.

(2) Hand-outs at exhibitions can help introduce new products to visitors and turn them into potential customers.

(3) Exhibitors' participation strategies include 3 steps: preparation, performance at the show, and assessment after the show.

(4) At the exhibition, when positive feelings are disappearing, regular briefings and teamwork can help cheer the team up.

(5) Politely filter out wrong-fit visitors and spare more time on the interested prospects.

Unit 8　Preparations for the MICE Profession

Lesson 1　Career Prospect of MICE

Section I

1. (1) T　(2) F　(3) F　(4) F　(5) T　(6) F　(7) T

3. (1) h　(2) e　(3) b　(4) i　(5) g　(6) d　(7) f　(8) j　(9) a　(10) c

Section III

1. Answer the following questions

(1) EU countries, Eastern Europe, the Middle East, Asia, the USA and Australia.

(2) Because of the low cost and being a new destination that can offer a new type of travel experience.

(3) Australia provides high quality products related to tourism.

(4) British Telecom's monopoly of telecommunications is hampering the UK's progress. This is due to slow adaptation of broadband facilities that determine access, and high cost.

(5) Staff in this industry lack professional training, which leads to poor service quality. What's more, they lack a sense of motivation as they are not sure about the career prospects.

(6) Other destinations; specific technologies; economic; human resource issues; infrastructure; marketing; and inadequate and/or incompatible statistics.

(7) A few. For example, to upgrade conference venue infrastructure and to develop new products; to invest in human resource development for the industry in order to become an attractive career option, and to improve employee motivation.

(8) Open-ended question

2. Translation

(1) The Asian conference products are good value due to the low cost and the many state-of-the-art conference venues available.

(2) After the Sydney 2000 Olympics, Australia was under the spotlight. It is also considered to be a very competitive conference market.

(3) The emergence of a series of modern communication technologies such as video conferencing reduces the need for face-to-face meetings.

(4) The high-level funding and support to MICE of other conference destinations has exerted great pressure on the British conference industry.

(5) In an increasingly competitive global conference marketplace, the British conference and meeting industry will have to adapt to change for survival.

(6) In order to promote further development of the MICE industry, the London Chamber of Commerce and Industry should lobby the government for funding and investment.

Lesson 2　Qualifications for the MICE Profession

Section Ⅰ

1. Answer the following questions

(1) Mr. Chan came to give a speech to prospective employees of exhibition companies.

(2) People who have the skill, experience and aptitude in conceptualizing, planning, managing and promoting an event.

(3) His major is English. Guangdong University of Foreign Studies.

(4) The language competence is quite necessary in this industry as the staff have to communicate with professionals from different backgrounds and cultures. Interpersonal relationships can be easily established without language barriers.

(5) To become an intern in an exhibition company; to get an accreditation for convention and exhibition interpreters; to attend the MPI training and get CMP global certification; to work in a transnational exhibition company.

(6) Exams for Convention and Exhibition Interpreters, Convention and Exhibition Strategists, Convention and Exhibition Designers, Convention and Exhibition Managers, Convention and Exhibition Organizers, etc.

(7) Certified Meeting Professional.

(8) It enables one to work everywhere in the world in MICE industry.

3. (1)c　(2)f　(3)j　(4)a　(5)h　(6)d　(7)g　(8)i　(9)b　(10)e

Section Ⅲ

1. Answer the following questions

(1) Not systematic, sporadic, lacking cooperation among various entities.

(2) Organizers of meetings and conventions, venue operator (e.g., convention centers, convention hotels), destination marketing organizations (e.g., CVBs, NTOs), supporting service providers (e.g., technical support firms), and independent PCOs.

(3) Interpersonal relationship, organizational, negotiation and communication skills, creativity, flexibility, and a team player mentality.

(4) They are career paths and opportunities designed to develop the expertise of personnel and encourage their retention in the industry; industry-specific education so that the industry is able to meet the demand for qualified and trained professionals; and accreditation and established code of ethics to ensure that the industry conforms to professional standards.

(5) Adult education is important to the growth of the MICE industry. This industry needs highly skilled workers as the industry has more new MICE facilities than before and becomes more complicated.

(6) North America.

(7) The programs are varied, either in-house or in cooperation with each other, industry partners, or universities.

(8) Courses taught include meeting planning, destination marketing, incentive travel, association management, convention facility management, and trade show operations.

2. Translation

(1) The size, scope and labor intensity of the global meetings and convention industry dictate the paramount importance of effective human resource policies and practices.

(2) A characteristic of employment in the MICE industry is the fact that traditionally no vocational training as such has been available and management positions are generally taken up by people from related industries.

(3) As the convention industry is essentially a service industry, with people taking a central role, it follows that interpersonal skills are critical for those working in the MICE sector.

(4) Reactive MICE organizations will be placed in a perilous situation in which they will have to "follow the leader", a potentially lethal business strategy in today's highly competitive environment.

(5) Managers in the meeting and convention industry will increasingly need to understand the fundamentals of adult education and learning to ensure an effective ROI to their customers.

(6) The demand for highly skilled employees is driven by the number of new MICE facilities being built throughout the world and increased sophistication of the industry and its customers.

参 考 文 献

[1] 吴云. 会展交际英语[M]. 上海：立信会计出版社有限公司，2004.

[2] 朱立文，胡竟扬. 会展英语文萃选读[M]. 北京：中国海关出版社，2004.

[3] 王铮. 会展英语[M]. 北京：高等教育出版社，2007.

[4] 丁衡祁，李欣，白静. 会展英语[M]. 北京：对外经济贸易大学出版社，2006.

[5] 戴光全，陈欣. 中国展览业的时空特点研究——基于因特网资料的内容分析[D]. 广州：华南理工大学经济与贸易学院会展经济与管理系.

[6] http://www.expoweb.com.

[7] http://www.interexpo.com.cn.

[8] http://www.tdctrade.com.

[9] http://www.cdesign.com.au.

[10] http://www.wtojob.com.

[11] http://www.2456.com/physhocos/download/SHOE2007.

[12] http://www.exhibitionworld.co.uk/featuredetails/152/crossing-oceans-expo-2012-yeosu-korea.

[13] http://www.exhibitionworld.co.uk/featuredetails/149/loud-and-proud-ecef-pulse-survey-results.

[14] http://www.cctv.com/travel/special/bts2004/20040706/102231.shtml.